HIKING IN CHINA

The Joys of Exploring the
Middle Kingdom on Foot

Dad, a friend of mine, Mable, published this book! Hoping you can make good use of it one day! Love, Sarah xo

Mable-Ann Chang

Hiking in China

Mable-Ann Chang

ISBN-13: 978-988-8552-70-2

© 2020 Mable-Ann Chang

TRAVEL/Asia/China

EB130

All rights reserved. No part of this book may be reproduced in material form, by any means, whether graphic, electronic, mechanical or other, including photocopying or information storage, in whole or in part. May not be used to prepare other publications without written permission from the publisher except in the case of brief quotations embodied in critical articles or reviews. For information contact info@earnshawbooks.com

Published by Earnshaw Books Ltd. (Hong Kong)

Contents

TAKING THE FIRST STEP   IX

PART I: THE HISTORY   1

Ministers, Monks, and Merchants   3
    Poet Scholars   3
    Pilgrimage Traditions   10
    Hiking Along the Silk Road   12

Foreign Travelers in China   15
    Robert Fortune   16
    George Morrison   18
    Isabella Bird   21
    Edwin Dingle   24

Modern Day Experiences   29
    The Chinese Park System   30
    An Unusual Hobby   30
    Red Tourism   31

PART II: THE PREPARATION   **33**

How to Get There   35

When to Go   39

Getting Around   45

On the Trail   53

PART III: THE HIKES   **65**
THE NORTH   67
The Beijing Area
    The Great Wall: Gubeikou   67
    Fenghuangling   71
    Yangtaishan and Jiufeng   73
    The Ming Tombs   75

Jiangsu
    The Nanjing City Wall   81

Gansu
    The Mogao Grottoes   87
    Zhangye   90

Hunan
    Wulingyuan   95

Hubei
    Wudangshan   99

THE SOUTH   105
Guangxi Zhuang
    The Longji Terraces   105
    Yangshuo   108

Guizhou
    Huangguoshu   113

Chongqing
    The Three Gorges of the Yangtze   119

Hong Kong
    The MacLehose Trail   125
    Victoria Peak Circle   125

THE WEST	131
Sichuan	
Emeishan	131
Ziuzhaigous	134
Yunnan	
Tiger Leaping Gorge	141
Shilin	144
THE EAST	149
The Shanghai Area	
West Lake	149
Moganshan	151
Anji Bamboo	154
Shandong	
Taishan	159
Penglai Vineyards	162
Anhui	
Huangshan	167
Jiangxi	
Lushan	173
Sanqingshan	176

HIKING IN CHINA

INTRODUCTION

Taking the First Step

Hiking in China is the experience of a lifetime. We have all seen photographs of the Great Wall, of the sparkling waters of the West Lake near the city of Hangzhou, and the sheer cliffs of the Gorges along the middle reaches of the Yangtze River. But nothing can match the experience of walking and hiking through such scenes. Walking is good for you, and so is hiking, and doing it in China is doubly good for you because of the incredible richness of the culture and the history through which you are passing.

When people think of China, they tend these days to think of Shanghai or Beijing—huge metropolises with bright lights and masses of people, often coated in a layer of smog. If they think of China's natural environment, if at all, they tend to picture pandas or bamboo, like screenshots from a Disney film. This book seeks to demonstrate that there is more to China than pandas, chopsticks and urban sprawl, and hiking and walking are a great way to experience it.

There is a rich tradition of appreciation for nature in China, and a history of hiking that stretches back thousands of years, making it an ideal location for those wanting to plan a trip to enjoy the open air.

From the gravity-defying trail across the Bridge of Eight Immortals in Anhui province, to the pathways of the Long March through Jinggangshan in Jiangxi province, walkways steeped in history are threaded across the country. In historic times, people travelled primarily for a purpose, rather than leisure. Monks sought the seclusion of mountains to gain enlightenment, merchants traversed the empire in pursuit of wealth, and soldiers scaled geography to attain territory and fame. These three categories provided the primary motivations for the hiking that has been done across China over the centuries.

Today's hikers in China are walking in the footsteps of these ancient travelers, surrounded by their legacy. In China, you will not only be passing on foot through some of the most magnificent scenery in the world, but also places that are steeped in millennia of history. There are very few places in the world where can you experience both at the same time. Yet hiking in China is not yet a mass pastime, although that number is steadily rising as travelers discover the abundance of trails and other walking itineraries, and more efforts are being taken to conserve and make accessible the country's scenic areas. Having boots on the ground allows hikers to discover China's unique culture and quirky elements in a direct way, and also enjoy many of those random moments that make traveling China so endearing.

This book contains hikes for the modest nature enthusiast, but also for the more experienced. It includes trails and walks in regions right across China, from the Stone Forest of Guizhou, to the Great Wall near Beijing and on to the glacial lakes of Jiuzhaigou in Sichuan. Almost all of the locations are just a few hours' train or plane ride from the major metropolises. Indeed, China's incredibly convenient internal connectivity is one of the main reasons why hiking here is now so feasible. The crystalline mountain lakes of Sichuan geographically are in another world, but they are

INTRODUCTION

less than four hours away from Beijing.

We would guess that three types of people in particular will be interested in this book. The first are those who love to travel and also have an avid interest in hiking, but live outside of China. The second group are people living in China, but who want to make hiking part of their experience here. Thirdly, Chinese people increasingly have an interest in getting away from the city and seeing more of their own country, and they may also appreciate the suggested walks and associated information.

Some of the trails and walks introduced are more appropriate for serious hikers, others for more casual walkers. This book tries to include a range of hikes that will appeal to all different classes of hikers with an interest in China, focusing on the classic sights that everyone should see. There is something for everyone. Just get out of the car and do some walking.

The book is divided into three parts. The first explains the history of hiking in China, as well as introduces some of the more colorful characters associated with perambulation in the Middle Kingdom. You will get a glimpse of what those erstwhile artists and explorers saw and experienced to provide context to the hikes and walks of modern China. The second section contains practical information on how to get to China, traveling within the country, and what gear hikers should consider carrying, both practical and electronic. It also offers some tips on interacting with Chinese people and culture, and the unique aspects of hiking in this vast and fascinating country. The third part of the book focuses on the specific hikes, divided into four cardinal regions and broken down further by province. It is designed so that hikers can find hikes near the area they will be traveling to easily, as well as helping you to decide on what you might find interesting. Special attention is given to the history behind the trails and places traversed, so that hikers and walkers can gain maximum richness from the experience.

Hiking in China is for a particular kind of traveler, the kind who wants to take the road less traveled and interface with the country and the culture on a deeper level, one that few foreigners and even Chinese people achieve. Enjoy your time in this spectacular place. You will create memories that will last a lifetime.

PART I
THE HISTORY

Ministers, Monks, and Merchants

ANCIENT HIKERS and walkers in the traditional Chinese world were a colorful and eclectic cast of characters. There were the scholars and officials were would take to the byways and paths for reflection and self-cultivation. Some were banished to the countryside as a result of some infraction at court, while others looking to escape the stifling atmosphere of the capital whiled away the days drinking wine and composed odes while strolling through the hills and valleys. Then there's were the religious-minded, Taoist and Buddhist monks and others seeking purification by visiting remote temples or secluding themselves in mountain retreats. And then there was money. Merchants and mercenaries took to the road looking for gold and glory. What follows are just three of the many stories of itinerants in old China.

Scholar Officials
With time on their hands, their basic needs were amply provided for and their highly-educated sophistication, the scholar-officials of China's old imperial world made an art out of meandering around the countryside. Their excursions are recorded in the paintings they would sometimes do and the poems they would write while reclining beside a running stream, crags towering above them, a courtesan

on hand to re-fill the wine cup. This golden world (for the few) was ripped apart by the wars and dislocations of the 19th century, and ended in 1911 with the end of the last dynasty. But many of them were astute travelers and records of their impressions have in many cases been passed down to the present day.

These literati often conveyed a deep sense of appreciation for the natural environment, and also its appropriate management. The philosopher Mencius, who lived around the year 300 BC, or about two hundred years after Confucius and three hundred before Jesus Christ, once advised King Huai of the state of Liang that there would always be an abundance of forest resources if people cut wood only at appropriate times. Forestry conservation starts here, but as you will see on traveling around China, King Huai's successors did not follow his advice — deforestation is one of China's biggest ecological problems.

Usually scholarly writings took the form of poetry, and some of the best examples were created during the Tang Dynasty in the 8th century AD and the Song Dynasty a couple of centuries later. The poems from these eras tend to have a straightforward structure, making them easy to understand and recite even a thousand years later. Many of the poems praise and celebrate the calm atmosphere of mountain and river scenery, or else bemoan the estrangement of the scholar official from the cultural hub that was the imperial court, employing natural imagery to convey their disconsolation.

Despite the hardships and the significant amount of time it entailed away from court life, many officials traveled extensively throughout the empire, and many obviously enjoyed it. Scholars were encouraged to "read ten thousand books and travel ten thousand *li,*" a *li* being a measure of distance about one-third of a mile or half a kilometer. Turning away from the bustle and intensity of city life, many of the literati were drawn to nature. In his poem "Green Mountain," written in the late 8th century, 1,200 or so years ago, the poet Li Bai says:

> You ask me why I dwell in the green mountains;
> I smile and make no reply for my heart is free
> of care
> As the peach-blossoms flow downstream and are
> fade into the unknown,
> I am in a world apart that is not among men.

Li Bai, who is China's most famous poet, traveled widely in central and western China, through many of the regions suggested in this book. He clearly gained enormous inspiration from nature, and was much influenced by Taoism, China's only home-grown "religion", although it is really a philosophy. At its heart, Taoism is about how human beings relate to the universe and to nature, and takes the view that we humans are puny and powerless and that things work best when humans show respect for the power of the universe and cleave to that power, which we can also call the way. The sense of humility encouraged by Taoism, which dates from 2,500 years ago, had a huge influence on the scholar class of which Li Bai was a member. The poetry of the literati travelers frequently reference the landscapes they pass through to convey the tone of their poems and to provide motifs for their underlying meanings. An astute scholar-gentleman would be able to hear a reference to a specific mountain or time of day and interpret the underlying history and emotional nuances.

Another interesting part of China's early hiking tradition is the literati painters. In the early Tang era, painting was still a professional occupation, and the turning point came only after the Mongols overran China in 1279 and set up the Yuan Dynasty. Although the Mongol imperial court absorbed many of the customs and procedures as well as the culture and Confucian values of the previous Chinese dynasty, many of the old elite found themselves either out of work, or they retired from court life to their countryside estates in protest. The practical result of this was that many former officials, people trained to wield an ink brush, were out in the mountains with a lot of free time on their hands.

These literati often lacked technical skills, but many of them had keen artistic sensibilities. It was during this period that the "Shan Shui" 山水 - literally 'mountain-water') style of painting was created and perfected. The paintings usually involve an ink-wash that was to some extent impressionistic and emphasized the artist's emotional reaction to Nature over literal depictions. The paintings generally focus on the glory of the natural scenery, and human beings and artificial structures, when present, and usually small and insignificant in the face of the grandeur of Nature.

The idealized literati artist of this era lived in a rustic area surrounded by Nature, far from the concerns of court life. These scholars would take their brushes into the hills looking for a landscape which inspired them, and then stop to capture its spirit in the sparse, monochromatic brush strokes of the style. Today, their works are considered to be the highest form of Chinese art. The scholar-painters are also perhaps the first of China's hikers to engage with Nature simply for pleasure, and one need only look at their creations to understand the awe they felt for the natural wonders to be found within China's landscape.

Xu Xiake

Perhaps the most eccentric example of the Chinese scholar-official is Xu Xiake (徐霞客), considered to be China's first geographer. Born in 1587 during the latter part of the Ming Dynasty, he was tall and wiry, and born with an incorrigible wanderlust that made his fellow literati consider him to be somewhat crazy. Xu Xiake spent 30 years traveling across China, and he was a meticulous observer and recorder of the natural world. Instead of merely describing his environment, he sought to understand it. He is thought to be the first to discover the source of the Xi River, as well as to determine that the Jinsha river network is the true source of the Yangtze River. He traveled from the icy peaks of Tibet and Sichuan, to the jungles of Guangxi and Yunnan, recording the terrain as he went. In total, Xu Xiake's works contain over four hundred thousand characters, an enormous body of detailed work for the time. His writing falls under the *youji wenxue* (遊記文學) category of Chinese literature, which literally means "travel writing." Xu's journals are exceptional for another reason—they were mostly written on the road, as opposed to from memory upon his return home.

If Xu Xiake had been American and asked about why

he climbed mountains, he might well have responded with George Mallory's famous three words, "Because it's there." As it is, what Xu actually recorded upon reaching one summit was, "I cried out in ecstasy, and could have danced out of sheer joy and admiration." Clearly, Xu's hikes brought him pleasure that all the hardships of living on the road could not dispel. The prosperity and highly-developed transportation and trading system of the Ming Dynasty allowed him to range the empire to his heart's content. Xu Xiake met with numerous setbacks and robberies, and often relied on the charity of monasteries and local officials in order to survive. But none of his struggles seem to have dampened his enthusiasm, as he spent most of his life either on the road or else planning his next expedition, until he died at the age of forty-nine from a disease contracted while out in the forests, most likely malaria. At the time, he was returning from his most ambitious expedition, to the foothills of the Himalayas, a life-long dream. In a world where scholar officials usually preferred the frenetic energy of court life or else bemoaned their estrangement from it in exile, Xu Xiake stands out for his genuine love of China's natural world.

Li Bai

Li Bai (701 A.D.—762 A.D.) is China's most famous poet, who lived and composed his great works during the Tang period, China's golden age of poetry. Every school child in China learns his poetry today, and every Chinese person can recite at least one of his verses. He was most likely born in Suyab, in present-day Kyrgyzstan, and spent his early years in Sichuan province, near Chengdu. Throughout his life he travelled an astonishing distance through much of the empire, including through Shandong, Xi'an, Jiujiang, Yelang, and Nanjing, and he wrote many of his best poems about the places he visited on the road, especially the areas around Chang'an, or present day Xi'an, then the capital of the empire. Much like the hikers of today, Li Bai enjoyed traveling for the journey itself, not the destination. His work exemplifies some of the finest travel poetry in the Chinese tradition, as well as the longest enduring in fame and popularity. Several of his works are included in this book.

Li Bai enjoyed both the favor of the court as an unofficial poet laureate, and also experienced capture and exile, the height of popularity and the depths of ignominy. At the age of 24, he left home to wander again for a time, before marrying and trying to settle down in Hubei province. But Li Bai was fundamentally a man with itchy feet, and soon he was back on the road. In 742 he stayed in Chang'an while attempting to become an official but no positions were forthcoming, although he *was* accepted into a society of court poets. Two years later he took up his travels again, and after a sequence of political miscalculations he was imprisoned at Jiujiang, and then banished to Yelang, a wild border region of southwest China, in today's Guizhou province. Eventually, after receiving an amnesty he returned to eastern China, where it is said he died by drowning when he drunkenly tried to capture the moon's reflection on the surface of a lake.

In accordance with his legend, much of Li Bai's poetry is about wandering about the countryside while intoxicated

THE HISTORY

on fine wine, but along with humor his work also consistently displays Taoist imagery and a striking imagination amidst scenic descriptions. A spontaneous and unpredictable person, Li Bai never stayed in one place or did one thing for very long, but he was entranced by life, nature, and the majesty of the natural landscape. In his poem "Hard Road," he writes:

> I want to cross the Yellow River, but ice blocks my way;
> I want to climb Mount Taihang, but snow fills the sky.
> In idleness I drop a hook into the azure creek,
> Suddenly I'm back in my boat, dreaming of distant places.
>
> Traveling is hard! Traveling is hard!
> So many forks in the road, which one to take?

Li Bai's ability to convey emotion simply and spontaneously is unrivaled. As Arthur Waley, the great translator of Chinese literature, pointed out, he was irresistibly drawn to the "wilder aspects of nature ... vast untenanted spaces, cataracts, trackless mountains and desolate ravines." He was on the road right until the end of his life.

Pilgrimage Traditions

Perhaps the most basic tradition of nature-walking in China is that of religious pilgrims. Pilgrimage in China is tied to hiking through the landscape, particularly the visiting of holy mountains. For more than two thousand years, monks and religious ascetics would seclude themselves in mountain retreats, seeking enlightenment through the calming presence of the natural world. For China, as for many other cultures around the world, high places were seen as being a locus of spiritual energy and enlightenment, and the famous peaks appear frequently in poetry and folk tales.

Buddhism and Taoism each have four sacred mountains scattered across the country, and local traditions often confer spiritual significance on local peaks. The Four Sacred Mountains of Buddhism include Wutaishan, Emeishan, Jiuhuashan, and Putoushan. Each has a patron bodhisattva to which the main shrine or temple is dedicated. For Taoism, meanwhile, there is Wudangshan, Longhushan, Qiyunshan, and Qingchengshan. But the mountains are not the exclusive province of one religion or another, and it is not uncommon to see shrines dedicated to Buddhist and Taoist statuary and deities side-by-side.

Xuan Zang

The most famous pilgrim in Chinese history is Xuan Zang, also called Tangsengm, who according to legend traveled from the capital of the Chinese empire, then Chang'an (today's Xi'an in the northwest of the country), westwards over deserts and southwards over the mountains to India to get the sacred Buddhist sutras to bring enlightenment to the Chinese people. This monk was an actual historical figure, a scholar and a traveler who lived in the 7th century AD during the early Tang Dynasty and he really did travel to India. The story is the basis of one of the most popular

THE HISTORY

classical Chinese novels entitled *Journey to the West* (西游记), in which the monk is instructed by Buddha to make the journey. She provides him with several traveling companions including the Monkey King, a super-powered monkey named Sun Wukong who is the most popular character in Chinese literature. Clever and mischievous, the Monkey King is forced to assist the monk after getting caught stealing fruit from heaven. The real Xuan Zang inspired many pilgrimages by Chinese Buddhist believers over the centuries, although traveling to religious sites such as the Longmen Grottoes or the Leshan Giant Buddha became a common practice, for monks and for laity. It remains so today. Even if it simply meant spending a couple months on a mountain retreat in quiet contemplation, hiking in holy places became a popular activity for those with either the time and money, or sufficient religious fervor. With the rise of the middle class in the modern day, Chinese people have begun to take up walking these old trails again, some for religious reasons and some out of simple interest.

Hiking Along the Silk Road

The most famous route in all of China is certainly the Silk Road. The phrase is actually a misnomer, as what it refers to is a network of trading routes that stretched across central and south Asia. The name was only coined in 1877 by Ferdinand von Richthofen, a German adventurer who made seven expeditions to China from 1868 to 1872 and for sure did a lot of hiking. The so-called Silk Road routes were critical to the exchange of goods and culture from at least the 2nd century B.C. during the Han Dynasty until the 15th century A.D. when the Ottoman Empire effectively closed off many of the trade routes.

One of the most prominent routes originated at Chang'an, the capital of the Tang and many other dynasties, and the home of the terracotta warriors who guard the tomb of China's first emperor. The Silk Road routes stretched 6,400 kilometers west across the mountains and deserts to the Mediterranean. Traders typically didn't traverse the entire route, but simply moved between settlements trading their goods, but there is evidence that Europeans made it to China, possibly but not certainly, including Marco Polo. From the west came wool, wine, glass, and precious metals, and from the east heading westwards went silk, tea, spices, and porcelain. The paths of the merchants were beaten into the earth over the centuries, and are still used for transportation and for recreation today. Three of the hiking areas included in this book have ties to the Silk Road—Dunhuang in Gansu, Shilin in Yunnan, and Mt. Emei in Sichuan.

Foreign Travelers in China

THE HISTORY of foreigners traveling to China is almost as old as the civilization. Most came for trade along maritime trade routes and the Silk Road. The most famous of these travelers is Marco Polo, whose account of China is heavily dramatized. In fact, it is uncertain he ever made it to China. In 1757, the Manchu Dynasty limited trade with foreigners to the single southern port of Canton, currently known in English as Guangzhou. The rest of the country was closed to access from the West. That changed at the end of the first Opium War in 1842, with the signing of the first of the unequal treaties, the Treaty of Nanking. The agreement forced China to abolish the Canton System and open additional ports to foreign merchants. Foreign merchants were allowed to deal directly with Chinese officials instead of relying on intermediaries, and missionaries were allowed to spearhead their gospel. Suddenly, China was open to the outside world.

Merchants, soldiers, and missionaries began to enter China, eager to win wealth, explore the unknown and find converts to Christianity. Western explorers were fascinated by a country that had been closed for so long, documenting a culture at the center of one world from the perspective of a culture at the center of another. The following four individuals were among the first to journey beyond the treaty ports and into China's interior, and the accounts they wrote of their travels formed the basis on which European audiences came to view China.

Robert Fortune

Robert Fortune was a Scottish botanist who made three trips to China to collect rare plants and bring them back to the West. His first expedition commenced in 1843 under the employment of the Royal Horticultural Society, a mere year after the Treaty of Nanking and the end of the first Opium War.

His first account of his travels, *Three Years' Wanderings in the Northern Provinces of China*, published in 1847, brought him to the attention of the East India Trading Company, the British company that dominated trade in East Asia. The EITC was seeking to smuggle tea plants out of China to India because the English had become addicted to tea and China was the only source of the leaves used to brew it. Timing was of the essence. If the British could produce tea in their colonies, they could end China's monopoly. Whoever managed to win the horticultural war first would have a titanic advantage. In light of this situation, it was Robert Fortune, the botanist from Berkshire, on whom the EITC placed their hopes. They offered him £500 per year to steal the best-kept secrets of China.

Unaware that the fate of two empires rested on his shoulders, Fortune set out for the tea terraces of Zhejiang and Anhui in 1847, equipped with a new-fangled glass contraption called the Wardian Case to preserve the precious seedlings. The grueling journey from Hangzhou was made by river and on foot, and to avoid suspicion Fortune shaved his hair and attached a fake queue, explaining his thickly-accented Chinese by pretending he was from a faraway province. In a second book in which he chronicled these adventures, *A Journey to the Tea Countries of China* published in 1852, Fortune describes his travels:

> "As I went far inland, and visited many districts almost unknown to Europeans, I now venture to lay an account of my travels and their results before the public. Blessed with a sound constitution and good health, I cared little for luxuries, and made light of the hardships of a traveller's life. New scenes, new countries, and new plants were day-by-day spread out before me and afforded gratification of the highest and purest kind. And even now, when on a different side of the globe and far removed from such scenes and such adventures, I often look back upon them with feelings of unalloyed pleasure."

Fortune's mission was successful. Traveling to regions that were supposedly still off-limits to Europeans after the first Opium War, such as Jiangsu, Fujian, and Guangdong provinces, he purchased many examples of the coveted black and green tea plants and then smuggled them out of China in his miniature glass greenhouses, along with the expertise necessary to nurture them. The East India Company gleefully began mass-cultivation of the plants in India in 1851, sparking an economic disaster for China that hastened the outbreak of the second Opium War.

Fortune seems to have never fully realized his impact on China or his contributions to that war. He visited China a third time and wrote two more books about his experiences, *A Residence Among the Chinese* as well as *Yedo and Peking*, published in 1857 and 1863 respectively. To Robert Fortune, his legacy was a few dozen beautiful flowers and shrubs that he introduced to the gardens of Europe, appropriately giving them the Latin species name *fortunei*. It was a humble legacy for a man whose adventures hiking through China's interior had such a profound impact on history.

George Ernest Morrison

Another man eager to take advantage of China's opening was George Morrison, a man of many coats. As a young man in Australia, he walked alone from north to south, 650 miles across the desert to Adelaide, and then created new adventures for himself in New Guinea, Spain, and many other places, often working as a doctor. He arrived in Shanghai in 1894, and the next year went on a trek across China and Burma, most of it on foot, narrated in his book *An Australian in China*. In his own words, his journey was "taken by one who spoke no Chinese, who had no interpreter or companion, who was unarmed, but who trusted implicitly in the good faith of the Chinese." Like Fortune, he avoided suspicion by wearing a hat with a queue attached.

The trip was only the beginning of a long career in China, highlighted by the Boxer Rebellion in 1900, when was correspondent for the *Times* of London and for a time arguably the most famous journalist in the world. Morrison had a complicated relationship with China. He arrived quite happy to admit to being prejudiced against the Chinese, yet he went on to become an advisor to the last man to be named as Emperor of China, Yuan Shikai (he died before he could formally ascend the throne) and advisor to the president of the new Chinese republic. Amazingly, he represented China at the Versailles talks that reset the world after World War I. He wrote:

> "I went to China possessed with the strong racial antipathy to the Chinese common to my countrymen, but that feeling has long since given way to one of lively sympathy and gratitude, and I shall always look back with pleasure to this journey, during which I experienced, while traversing provinces as wide as European kingdoms, uniform kindness and hospitality, and the most charming courtesy."

Morrison would have cut quite a figure striding through the Chinese countryside, with his shabby Chinese-style clothes but imperious air , followed by hired servants and unable to speak more than a few dozen words of the local language. Morrison describes himself on his travels in the following way:

> I was dressed as a Chinese teacher in a thickly-

wadded Chinese gown, with pants, stockings, and sandals, with Chinese hat and pigtail. In my dress I looked a person of weight. I must acknowledge that my outfit was very poor; but this was not altogether a disadvantage, for my men would have the less temptation to levy upon it. Still it would have been awkward if my men had taken it into their heads to walk off with my things, because I could not have explained my loss. My chief efforts, I knew, throughout my journey would be applied in the direction of inducing the Chinese to treat me with the respect that was undoubtedly due to one who, in their own words, had done them the "exalted honour" of visiting "their mean and contemptible country."

People with money and status did not walk in old China, they sat in a palanquin, or sedan chair, armed with two long poles running along each side which were carried by either two or four people. Morrison walked, because he said he could not afford a private sedan chair. However, he quoted the English traveler Edward Colborne Baber as saying that:

"No traveller in Western China who possesses any sense of self-respect should journey without a sedan chair, not necessarily as a conveyance, but for the honour and glory of the thing. Unfurnished with this indispensable token of respectability he is liable to be thrust aside on the highway, to be kept waiting at ferries, to be relegated to the worst inn's worst room, and generally to be treated with indignity, or, what is sometimes worse, with familiarity, as a peddling footpad who, unable to gain a living in his own country, has come to subsist on China."

Despite the lack of a palanquin, Morrison seemed to have no problem getting the respect he sought. Notwithstanding his cantankerous personality and limited vocabulary, he was a sharp observer, recording the people and things that crossed his path with directness and wit, if not always in a positive light. His account of walking through China in the 1890s is one of few of the era without a religious missionary slant, and his sardonic sense of humor makes his book as entertaining as it is enlightening.

Isabella Bird

Born in 1831 in Yorkshire, Isabella's chances of seeing much of the world seemed early in her life to be slim. A frail child who suffered frequent headaches and problems with her spine, Isabella was nevertheless encouraged by her doctors to get plenty of fresh air, and her father, a Church of England minister and botanist, encouraged her nascent love of nature. At the age of twenty-two, she took a ship across the Atlantic to visit family in America, and that journey kicked off an enthusiastic life of travel and writing. Isabella's relationship with China began briefly in 1878, but it wasn't until her final lengthy journey in 1897 that she truly became acquainted with the country, at 66 years of age. Isabella travelled up the Yangtze River, taking photographs and hanging them off the gunwales of the boat to dry. She loved journeying through the Chinese interior as much as she disdained the foreign enclaves, writing "my chief wish on arriving at a foreign settlement or treaty port in the East is to get out of it as soon as possible."

Normally, Isabella travelled by boat or by palanquin, but she enjoyed walking a great deal despite her age, much to the consternation of the bearers she had hired to assist her. She describes their confusion:

> "On another occasion in SZE CHUAN, when I left my chair and walked up a part of the colossal staircase by which the road is carried over the Pass of Shen Kia-chao, my bearers showed the construction they put on my doing so by asking, "Does the foreign woman think us not strong enough to carry her?"

Clearly, Isabella had a mind of her own. Her exploits earned her an international readership and the position of being the first woman elected to the Royal Geographic Society. Her two main works on China, *The Yangtze Valley and Beyond* published 1899, and a compilation of photographs, *Chinese Pictures: Notes on photographs made in China*, in 1900, were written after eleven previous volumes of travel writing had been published. They showcase her mastery of the genre, as well as her fascination with the experiences of ordinary Chinese people who she met on the road. In terms of her opinions on China, she was not unbiased, but neither was she overly critical or negative in her judgments. At times she demonstrated a sharp insight into the motivations of the colonial powers, including her native Britain, as in the following section:

> "In much talk about "open doors" and "spheres of influence" and "interest," in much greed for ourselves, not always dexterously cloaked, and much jealousy and suspicion of our neighbours, and in much interest in the undignified scramble for concessions in which we have been taking our share at Peking, there is a risk of our coming to think only of markets, territory, and railroads, and of ignoring the men who, for two thousand years, have been making China worth scrambling for. It may be that we go forward with 'a light heart,' along with other European empires, not hesitating, for the sake of commercial advantages, to break up in the case of a fourth of the human race the most ancient of earth's existing civilisations, without giving any equivalent."

At the turn of the 19th century, only thirteen brief years before the collapse of the Qing Empire, this statement was prescient. Isabella was unafraid to step out of the restricted life of a Victorian woman and experience China firsthand, even during a period when Westerners were not always welcomed. Isabella was interested in the local culture, in seeing what lay beyond the walls of the treaty ports, and she made her mark as one of the few foreigners, and women, to walk through the interior of China during the last days of the imperial era.

THE HISTORY

Edwin J. Dingle

Born in 1881 in Cornwall, Dingle first dipped his toes in Asia in 1900 when he became a journalist in Singapore, but his wanderlust eventually carried him to China. In 1909, he sailed to Shanghai, then up the Yangtze river to the city of Chongqing, and walked from there the provinces of Sichuan and Yunnan to Burma. In total he travelled about 2,500 kilometers in nine months, an impressive statistic considering how often he was ill and how the trip was made. His book, *Across China on Foot*, was published in 1911.

Dingle was proud of himself for this accomplishment and for eschewing the comforts of his peers, writing rather dryly that, "To travel in China is easy. To walk across China, over roads acknowledgedly worse than are met with in any civilized country in the two hemispheres, and having accommodation unequalled for crudeness and insanitation, is not easy." And yet Dingle did so, more closely relating him to the hikers of today in that respect than most of the other European adventurers in China of his day. Like Morrison, he spoke little Chinese, but Dingle delighted in the day-to-day experience of life on the road in China and in writing about it. In his own words, from his book:

> "My trip was undertaken for no other purpose. I carried no instruments (with the exception of an aneroid), and did not even make a single survey of the untrodden country through which I occasionally passed. So far as I know, I am

the only traveler, apart from members of the missionary community, who has ever resided far away in the interior of the Celestial Empire for so long a time. Most of the manuscript for this book was written as I went along — a good deal of it actually by the roadside in rural China."

The fact that Dingle wrote while he travelled was a particular point he wanted to drive home, as his account of his trip is so vivid that some of his peers accused him of embellishment. While this was a common occurrence in travel writing at the time, especially in books written post-journey, Dingle's narrative is plausible. Given his imagination and enthusiasm, his writing does have a fantastical, lyrical quality, but so do the places he visited. He wrote the following description while trekking through Yunnan:

"Passing over the stream — the Hsiang-shui Ho, I believe — I stepped out across the plain with one foot soaked, a pony having pulled me into the water as he drank. Peas and beans covered with snow adjoined a heart-breaking road which led up to a long, winding ascent through a glade overhung by frost-covered hedgerows, where the sun came gently through and breathed the sweet coming of the spring. From midway up the mountain the view of the plain below and the fine range of hills separating me from the capital was one of exceeding loveliness, the undisturbed white of the snow and frost sparkling in the

THE HISTORY

> sunshine contrasting most strikingly with the darkened waves of billowy green opposite, with a background of sharp-edged mountains, whose summits were only now and again discernible in the waning morning mist. Snow lay deep in the crevices. My frozen path was treacherous for walking, but the dry, crisp air gave me a gusto and energy known only in high latitudes."

Dingle had a deep love of hiking, particularly through the mountains, a love he put to good use during his travels through southern China. He also had a keen eye for the edifices and structures of bygone empires, and reconstructed for his readers what human activity must have looked like centuries before:

> "In a pass cleared out from the rock we halted and gained breath for the second ascent, surmounted by a dismantled watchtower. It has long since fallen into disuse, the sound tiles from the roof having been appropriated for covering other habitable dwellings near by, where one may rest for tea. The road, paved in some places, worn from the side of the mountain in others, was suspended above narrow gorges, an entrance to a part of the country which had the aspect of northern regions. The sun, tearing open the curtain of blue mist, inundated with brightness one of the most beautiful landscapes it is possible to conceive. A handful of Dublin Fusiliers with quick-firing rifles concealed in the hollows of

the heights might have stopped a whole army struggling up the hillsides. But no one appeared to stop me, so I went on."

Just as in Dingle's day, visitors to Yunnan today can experience the sharp-edged mountains cloaked in mist, and the relics of watchtowers from a bygone era. While even more convenient modes of transportation than donkeys and palanquins exist today, hikers can also take paths not much changed from when Dingle walked them more than a hundred years ago.

Modern Day Experiences

TRAVELING ON FOOT in China in the modern sense truly began with the Communist Revolution, and the Long March, when in 1934 and 1935 communist rebels walked thousands of miles to escape efforts by Chinese government forces to annihilate them. Then came the Japanese invasion in 1937, the end of World War II in 1945, and the Chinese civil war which ended with the communists winning in 1949. That and the Korean War and later various political campaigns led to mainland China being basically closed to the outside world for decades. Foreign adventurers were not welcome, and most Chinese were poor, and few had the opportunity or inclination to do any travel. This changed in 1979, when the country started to open up again, and even more so in the 1980s and 1990s as the economy modernized. China's markets began to grow, and with prosperity was born a middle class. Foreign eccentrics were able to visit the country once again, and in the 1990s foreign backpackers and hikers started to strike out into the relatively unknown, the back blocks of China once more. They brought with them a different idea about what recreation means, and the new Chinese middle class took note. Today, hiking is on the rise, as is interest in Chinese culture and heritage.

THE HISTORY

The Chinese Park System

China first began establishing national parks in the 1980s, with about 250 designated in the first group. The system was developed on lines similar to those that propelled American conservationism, namely protection of precious ecosystems and the promotion of national nature tourism. While China's system looks good on paper, there is still a wide gap between goals and local implementation. China's natural preserves face many challenges, including in some cases mining and waste dumping in protected areas, as well as decades of logging and overgrazing. The country has also struggled with severe deforestation brought on by rapid industrialization and urbanization. Despite these challenges, China's park system is evolving and maturing, especially as more and more tourists gain interest in visiting scenic areas. Rapid depopulation of mountain farming regions is also creating opportunities for returning land to nature and creating larger national parks. More protection rules are being instituted and more money is going to conservation and preservation, as well as into tourism development. Today, in addition to the original parks, China has 31 UNESCO Geoparks, 16 Heritage Sites, and nearly 500 nature reserves, along with locally protected areas. These sites contain some of the most fantastic wonders of the natural world anywhere on the planet, and more and more people are enjoying them every year.

An Unusual Hobby

Up until very recently, Chinese people did not think of hiking, at least in the American or European sense, as a hobby or even necessarily an enjoyable activity. Part of what makes

Chinese national parks such an enigma to Western hikers is the behavior of most of the Chinese tourists who visit them—they tend to stay in groups and only stop at the scenic overlooks accessible by road to snap photos. In all but the most crowded of scenic areas, a few minutes' walking down one of the trails will separate the hiker from the vast majority of other visitors. Despite this herd proclivity, real hiking is on the rise in China, especially among the younger generation who, with the rise in prosperity, now have the time and money as well as the inclination to get outside the cities and into nature. Small hiking groups have popped up around China, conducting small hikes and camping trips in forested areas. While most Chinese park visitors will still prefer to get on and off a tour bus, some are beginning to explore the country's natural wonders in a more holistic way. As such, foreign hikers are less of an oddity than they were twenty or even ten years ago.

Red Tourism

Of course, the most quintessential of all Chinese "hikes" is the Long March, begun in 1934 by the communist guerrilla forces of 300,000 or so people, of whom only 40,000 made it to the destination of Yan'an in Shaanxi Province. In 370 days they traveled approximately 9,000 kilometers, most of them starting in the south in Jiangxi Province, circling west and then north across some of China's most difficult terrain, fleeing Chinese government forces. Today this March has reached legendary status. Many of the buildings and hideouts where Mao and other Communist party members rested are still preserved today, and these sites and other associated with the rise of the Communist Party

THE HISTORY

have become the basis of a thriving business nicknamed "red tourism." Companies sometimes have employees march along part of the original route as a team-building exercise. Many more people flock to sites and roads along the path out of a sense of patriotism or an interest in history. Red tourism has expanded beyond the route of the original Long March to include any of the places the communist leaders stayed at or where they gave famous speeches. Two locations with hikes in this book, Taishan and Lushan, in particular are associated with China's modern history and shaped the direction of the country. Other important locations are Yingshan and Jianggangshan, where several revolutionary battles took place. As you explore China, don't be surprised to encounter monuments to China's communist history.

PART II
PREPARING TO HIKE

Getting to China

Travel Documents

In order to enter China, you will need some kind of visa, most likely a tourist visa. Citizens of Canada, the U.S., and the U.K. can currently acquire a multiple-entry tourist visa that is good for 10 years, with 60 days maximum per visit. However, regulations change frequently, so check the website of the Chinese consulate with jurisdiction over the area in which you live for specific information. Obtaining the proper documents and submitting them to a Chinese consulate may take a significant amount of time, so try and start the process at least a month in advance of when you plan to travel. Alternatively, instead of doing the paperwork yourself, consider hiring a visa service company to handle the application process for you, for a fee. There are many such services available, so shop around and find one that handles China visas. Travel agencies also sometimes can assist you with this process.

If you are traveling to either Xinjiang or Tibet, you will need to apply for a special permit on top of your regular visa. In order to get this permit, you must first purchase a visit package with a tour group company, which will then help you obtain permission. It typically takes at least two weeks to get a permit on top of the visa, so factor this into your scheduled timeframe.

PREPARING TO HIKE

When you travel to China, it is a good idea to print out all your documents and carry them with you on the plane, as well as the address of your hotel in Chinese for your taxi driver. Try and obtain a letter signed by your physician for any medications you may be taking, and their business card. And beyond that, follow common sense and the regulations of international airlines.

Immunizations
Depending on where you are coming from, you need to keep in mind that strains of bugs and illnesses in various parts of Asia are going to be different from your home varieties. Look up the areas you plan to be hiking, and follow CDC and other major health organizations' guidelines on what immunizations you need. A doctor that practices travel medicine can assist you. Of course, make sure your vaccinations are up to date. Few things are more unpleasant than becoming ill on vacation in a foreign country, especially if you are away from hospitals and the more densely-populated areas. Naturally, your body will need to acclimate to the new environment, but that doesn't mean you have to struggle through a preventable illness first.

GETTING TO CHINA

When to Go

Geography and Seasonal Weather

By landmass, China is the third-largest country in the world, second only to Russia and Canada. Predictably, this means the country's climate and geography has a vast degree of variation. Along the coasts are subtropical and even tropical jungles, the air thick with humidity and insects. If you look at a topographical map, you will notice that the east is marked by fertile hills fed largely by two of Asia's greatest rivers, the Yellow River to the north and the Yangtze River to the south. The climate in the region to the south of the Yangtze River valley tends to be relatively subtropical, with mild winters and hot, wet summers. To the north of the Yangtze, the land becomes dryer and the winters much colder. The coast regions of the east and the south are the most densely populated, but the cradle of Chinese civilization is in the Yellow River valley further north. In the southwest, the land rises sharply upwards, shaped by the tectonic forces that created the Tibetan Plateau and the Himalayas. This region tends in its higher areas to be dry, alpine, with heavy snows and cool summers. In the north of China, the mountains break into sharp ridges, and then sand. The Gobi Desert and its cousins blanket much of northern China and southern Mongolia, with sparse vegetation, hot days and cold nights.

The hiking destinations in this book are split into four regions, for convenience.

> The **northern section** encompasses the area connected by Beijing, Gansu and Hubei provinces, and Nanjing.
>
> Shanghai marks a transition to the **east section**, which stretches from Shandong province in the north down through Jiangxi and Anhui. This coastal region has the most humid and hot weather, as well as the densest population. Hiking areas here tend to be heavily touristed but readily accessible and layered in history.
>
> The **southern section** includes hikes in Guangxi, Guizhou, and Chongqing, as well as the city of Hong Kong. These areas contain some of China's best-known scenic imagery.
>
> **The west** includes the provinces of Sichuan and Yunnan. The scenic areas here include some of China's most rugged terrain, and also are close to the birthplace of the three rivers that feed the Sichuan basin and the rest of China. An astute reader will notice that these regions are not the farthest to China's west. Xinjiang, Qinghai, and Tibet have been excluded from this book due to their remoteness from the most populated areas and transportation hubs. Hiking in those regions can be more difficult and challenging, and if you wish to pursue it, it is best to consult more specific sources.

WHEN TO GO

Each hiking section of the country has its own benefits and challenges. When considering where to go and at what time of year, think about what kind of hiking you are accustomed to and interested in, and what the weather will be like when you visit. Unless you specifically want to hike through the snow or a rainstorm, avoiding the north in the winter months and coastal areas in summer is not a bad plan. Always check the yearly average temperature and the weather forecast before packing. Pay particular attention to factors such as wind and humidity, which can make otherwise temperate conditions unbearable. Predictably, spring and autumn are the two mildest seasons for visiting and hiking around China, although travelers should also be aware of the monsoon season, which can hit the southern coastal areas from April through June, and more northern coastal areas from July through August. Southern China in particular receives heavy rainfall during this period.

Public Holidays

While festivals are a great time to experience Chinese culture, it would be best to avoid traveling around these dates, especially the Chinese Lunar New Year (Spring Festival)—which usually falls in late January or early February—and National Holiday in October. Many Chinese people will be traveling back to their hometowns around these dates, overloading the transit system in what is the world's largest periodic migration. Tickets will be expensive and difficult to purchase, and stations will be even more crowded than they are usually. Some restaurants and businesses will also be closed. The official holiday schedule with exact dates is published by the Chinese government every year and is

PREPARING TO HIKE

readily available online, so make sure to check your dates and see if they coincide with any major holidays before you book your tickets.

Pollution
Many hikers will understandably be concerned about the air quality in China, which is considered among the worst in the world. Reasonable precautions should be taken. Winter is usually the worst season for pollution, especially in the north where winter is bitter and weather patterns can keep the smog blanket close to the ground. However, pollution levels are fickle and can be dense or light at any time of the year. During warmer times of the year and in the less densely populated areas, visitors typically need not be as concerned with the air quality, especially as they move away from the big metropolis centers.

Check the average annual pollution levels for the areas you plan to visit before you leave, and if you can see the murk, then check regularly during your trip too. If you plan to be in the city or in areas where smog is heavy, then invest in a facemask. Be sure the mask fits snugly on your face, and filters p2.5, which are small pollutant particles that can bury themselves deep in your lung tissue. Look for a product rated N95 or N99, which refers to the percentage of air the mask filters. Some of the best brands currently on the market are the Cambridge ProMask, Vogmask, Respro, and 3M. With these precautions, you can enjoy your trip safely.

WHEN TO GO

Getting Around China

Accommodation

In general, it is recommended that you stay in a hotel or hostel when you are in China. There are two main reasons for this. The first is that foreigners are required to register their address within 24 hours of entering the country, and for every night during which they are in China. Hotels and hostels booked through reputable services will scan your passport and send your information to the relevant public bureau automatically, so that you don't have to go to the police station in person. Failure to register can result in fines and possibly detention. Because of this, it is technically illegal to camp out in the open in China, as there is no way to register the address of a tent. The second reason camping in China is discouraged is because it is simply more dangerous than the alternative. Monkeys and other wild animals will have little trouble or consciousness about dismantling your temporary abode in the pursuit of food. Fabric also provides little protection against curious or malicious strange beasts. Tempting as it might be, it's best to leave your tent at home and simply book a room.

Planes

The four main airlines are Air China, Southern Airlines, Eastern Airlines, and Hainan Airlines. Be aware that as in many major cities around the world, there are two airports in a number of important Chinese metropolises, and be sure to go to the right one. In Shanghai, there are Hongqiao and Pudong airports, and in Beijing there are Beijing Capital and Beijing Nanyuan, with a third on the way. Be sure your taxi or train takes you to the correct airport and also the correct terminal, as they are often a significant distance from each other. If possible, try to fly on days when the weather is good—Chinese airlines are more likely than their western counterparts to ground flights due to rain. And booking flights early in the day is a good strategy. Delays for a variety of reasons are common, and flight times can slip during the day, but the early flights are usually on time.

Flight regulations do change, as do security requirements. Standard flying restrictions apply, with a few extra more particular to China. Lithium batteries are not allowed in checked luggage, and carry-on is restricted to two battery chargers per passenger, each of no more than 10,000 mAh capacity. Liquids and gels in carry-on as you go through security must be less than 100 ml each, with a maximum of 1 liter in total. Some regulations are temporary, and some are not intuitive—flyers are often asked to remove umbrellas from their carry-ons so they can be scanned separately at security. The rule here is simply to follow signs and the gestures of the security agents, be polite, and always have your documentation with you.

In terms of luggage, it is common for Chinese flyers to wrap their suitcases in giant sheets of plastic to discourage theft and enhance identifiability. While international travelers need not necessarily go to this extreme, it is advisable to use luggage that can be locked. If you are transferring from an international flight to a domestic flight, be sure to check the luggage weight requirements for the ticket you have purchased, and expect to be allowed smaller sizes than in the U.S. or in Europe, as domestic flights can be restricted to 20kg (but judgments are usually made on size rather than weight).

Trains
China is now covered by a vast network of fast, convenient, and comfortable railway lines. You can travel almost anywhere in a few hours, usually for much cheaper than the price of a plane ticket. The high-speed rail network runs at standard speeds of 300 kilometers per hour, and they are almost always on time. Railway stations in China are comparable to airports, in that the security apparatus is similar, and there are large waiting areas where passengers sit before the gates to the actual platforms open. You can also usually purchase snacks and quick meals from the shops and vending booths in the stations, but the food is often overpriced, so consider bringing food and drinks with you. One popular option is cup noodles, as there is usually boiling tap water available near the restrooms. A food trolley goes up and down the aisle offering noodles, drinks and other edibles.

It's fairly straightforward to buy train tickets at a station, but for the purposes of planning it is recommended to buy in advance. When tickets become available for purchase varies by their type, but most sales open a month in advance. Some of the more popular website choices for booking train tickets are trip.com, China Highlights and China DIY travel. When you purchase your train tickets through an agency, you'll get a confirmation with a reference number. Take this booking reference and your passport to the ticket office at the station to pick up your tickets. If you are leaving the same day, try to arrive early, as lines may be long, especially during the holidays or special events. But the lines tend to move quickly – the whole process is remarkably smooth and efficient considering the huge number of people being processed.

Cars

Taxis are readily available in major and minor cities, but look up the regular fares beforehand so you have some idea what the standard rate should be. Taxis should always have a functioning meter and a picture of the driver with their license information inside the cab, and the driver should give you a receipt when the trip is complete. The reason for taking this is that if you have any problems during the journey or forget something in the back of the cab, you can call the company and report it. Be careful of fraud at popular locations like airports and tourist spots. At transportation centers, namely train stations and airports, always find and use the official queue and ignore the entreaties of touts, no matter how long the taxi queue is. Again, such lines tend to move faster than you expected.

If you can speak Chinese to some extent, you can hire a car and driver in different parts of China. Different cities have different companies offering different rental rates, so do your research and read reviews ahead of time. Think about how traffic might influence your plans. For example, rush hour in Beijing will significantly slow traffic more than in other places. If you rent a car for an eight-hour itinerary but get caught in traffic, you might spend two hours staring at the same few blocks. Planning is key.

It is not advisable that you drive yourself. Among other reasons, driving in China is only legal with a Chinese driver's permit, as international permits are not accepted. Besides that, most of the signs, signals, and road markings are in Chinese, and the driving culture is unique and takes some getting used to. You are better off hiring an experienced local driver to take you where you need to go.

Phone Apps

Apps are a convenient and sometimes necessary way to interface with the Chinese world, which is heavily integrated into mobile phone culture. In terms of language apps, Pleco is unequivocally the best dictionary app on the market for Chinese-English. Its straightforward software is easy to use, and also free. You may also want to download the Google Translate app, especially if your Mandarin is basic. In terms of getting around, DiDi ChuXing (滴滴出行) is the Uber of China, and is available in English. Google Maps is blocked in China and will not work unless you download a VPN, discussed in more detail below. Many Chinese people use Baidu Maps (百度地图), which is a good substitute, but best if you can read and type some Chinese. Apple Maps is a third alternative, and in China uses data from the app Autonavi (高德导航), which is popular among drivers. In terms of roads and trails in less populated areas, many hikers in China find Maps.me useful, and you can also download data and access the maps offline.

In terms of general travel and booking planes, trains, and hotels in China, the app trip.com, is currently the best

PREPARING TO HIKE

resource on the market. The interface is available in English, and is easy to use. For booking train tickets, the app China Train Booking is also popular and efficient. Another app that hikers may find useful is Air Matters, formerly called China Air Quality Index, which provides up-to-date and reliable information on the air quality in a long list of China locations, along with recommendations about whether to wear a facemask and exercise guidelines.

If you are a foreigner looking to travel in China for the first time, be aware that many websites, especially those that run on a Google platform, are blocked in China, including phone apps. If you wish to access Facebook, Gmail, Dropbox, major news outlets, and selected other sites while in China, you should download a reputable VPN before you leave. VPNs, or virtual private networks, use encryption and network protocols. When it comes to which VPN services have the best access and value changes, it's best to check online with travelers who have previously been to China for recommendations. Resist the temptation to download a free service—it will not work as well as a paid subscription and will not have comparable customer support. Spend a little extra on one of the big names, such as Astrill, ExpressVPN or NordVPN. Be sure to download and set up your service before entering China, as it is difficult once you arrive.

GETTING AROUND CHINA

On the Trail

Gear

Pick your gear to suit the conditions in which you are hiking. For example, what you pack for the gorges of the Yangtze River will be different than for the deserts of Inner Mongolia. But in any case, make sure you have a sturdy, lightweight pack and quality hiking boots. You can purchase hiking boots in China, but the construction may not be the same as in the U.S. or Europe, especially in terms of arch and ankle support. You needn't pack any special equipment that you would not bring for similar conditions in any other part of the world with a similar environment. The exception to this is American toiletries such as deodorant and sunscreen. Chinese products tend to have different chemicals and often skin-whitening agents in them, so it is best to bring a supply of the brand you prefer from home. Also, make sure when you head out on the trail that you have own supply of tissues with you as squat toilets are common and restrooms tend to lack paper.

Some travelers like to use mosquito-repellent wrist and ankle bands. As much of China is in a subtropical climate zone and therefore has many, many insects, you may wish to purchase some of these. However, bug spray is also readily available in China. it is also worth considering bringing an eye mask and a set of ear plugs, as privacy is

PREPARING TO HIKE

virtually non-exist, with hostels tending to have thin walls.

When planning your wardrobe, sweat-blocking fabrics are the best, as well as ones that dry quickly. People in Asia do not generally use drying machines, and clothes washed at a laundromat or in the sink will take longer to dry I'd you are in a part of China that is humid. Bring a hat with a brim, and a lightweight scarf for hiking in windy conditions. For females, try to choose clothes that cover your shoulders and avoid low necklines, as Chinese fashion tends to be more modest in these areas than Western fashion. A passport pouch that you can wear under your clothing is also a good idea. When traveling, your passport is your most valuable possession—do everything you can to make sure it isn't lost or stolen.

Electric outlets vary to some extent by location in China, but the electric voltage is 220V. It's best to purchase a universal adapter. You may also want to invest in some kind of waterproof mobile phone case. Power banks are almost a necessity in China considering how much people use their phones, so purchase one to make sure you are not caught without a translator or a map. Airport security at all airports in China has a limit of two power banks per traveler, and really big power banks – over 20,000mAh – will be denied passage. Two 10,000mAh battery packs is a good balance and is probably enough.

In America, it is common for backpackers to bring water filters on the trail if they are planning multi-day excursions. In China, however, all the water you drink should be bottled. In a surprisingly wide range of locations you will find a little shop or stall where bottled water is for sale, usually at less than RMB 5 a bottle. Do not trust an American filter to be of much use here. Some visitors to China also bring activated charcoal tablets. If you have a sensitive stomach, these tablets can absorb toxins and help your system digest foods that you may not be used to eating at home.

Readers will note that we have not included maps in this book. This is for two main reasons — China changes fast and maps of even something as allegedly timeless as trails can become out of date, and also because detailed maps of everything are now available on the internet for viewing on the inevitable mobile phone being carried by our readers. To get the best and most up-to-date information about a particular trail, ask someone who has hiked it before, or pick up the most current maps from your hotel or hostel, or the scenic area entrance gate. In addition, remember to always take photos of any signs you encounter at the trailhead. Remember that while phone apps are a good resource, they may not locate you accurately or reveal potential setbacks or dangers.

Avoiding Crowds

Most hikers prefer to avoid tourist spots and large crowds of people. Part of the enjoyment of nature, after all, comes from its tranquility, as opposed to the hectic atmosphere of urban life. However, travelers in China should understand that the country is an intensely crowded place, and many people will probably be visiting the same places as you. It's very hard to be alone in China, and entirely possible to believe, as you watch the streams of people in the most inaccessible places, that the country has a population of 1.4 billion – at least. With this in mind, there are a few ways to avoid becoming lost in a crowd. The first is to arrive at your destination early in the day. Most people on vacation will be getting a later start, so a good way to avoid the masses is to go as early as possible. Most scenic areas are open by 8am, and some even earlier. Another tip is to move as quickly as possible beyond the entrances and photo spots. Many Chinese tourists visit parks only long enough to eat, take some pictures, and get back on a tour bus. By going beyond the advertised locations and away from the tour groups, you will greatly decrease the number of people around you. In a similar vein, go on longer hikes or trails, and take side routes up mountains instead of the main road. While you shouldn't go off-trail completely, longer paths are likely to be much less busy. Beyond these tips, simply get comfortable with your neighbors. People are part of what China is, and if you are in the country you are bound to rub shoulders at times with the billion-plus population.

And that is okay.

Etiquette and Customs
The first rule of international travel is to recognize that you are in someone else's backyard. As a result, it is incumbent on the hiker in China to behave in a friendly and respectful manner. As you move farther from the cities, and depending on what you look like, the more of a peculiarity you will become. If you look foreign, people will naturally be interested in you and what you are doing. Visiting China does have the advantage that the country on balance is a very safe place to travel. Guns are unknown in society and all law and order-related issues are tightly controlled. Public drunkenness is rare and frowned upon by the society at large. If you do happen to find yourself in a negative

situation, it is most likely to arise from miscommunication. The exception involves a few touts and scam-artists on the streets of some of the main cities, particularly Shanghai, who might try to lure you into a restaurant and then present you with a bill for a huge sum, but that has nothing to with hiking. This is as good a place as any to pass on another piece of advice – don't have anything to do with any illegal recreational drugs while you are in China. One place you don't want to do any hiking is in a Chinese prison yard.

As with most activities in China, the ability to speak the language to some degree will be a great help when you are hiking. it will help with ordering food, reading signs, asking for directions, and doing a number of other activities. It will also help should you need immediate assistance during your trip, especially in an emergency. However, many visitors to China know little or no Chinese, and they get by just fine. In fact, knowing some Chinese can in some circumstances be worse than knowing no Chinese at all, as people are more likely to assume you understand exactly what is coming out of your mouth and also understand exactly what is coming out of theirs. If there is a misunderstanding, people may become more easily offended. This does not mean you should throw learning Chinese to the wind and come to China completely unprepared. It's a good idea to pick up a Mandarin 101 manual, and also learn to read some Chinese words. But while learning a few words and phrases may help you, pay attention to all the other facets that go into communication. Goodwill and a big smile are more important and will take you farther than you may think.

If you run into communication problems, look around for someone you can ask for help. Students in China all study

English and will may be able to speak a little of it, or will have a smartphone that can translate. When you are talking, speak slowly and clearly, whether in English or Chinese. Smile, and keep a positive facial expression. How you present yourself is more important than what you actually say, and can help smooth over blunt or offensive language if it is clear you do not mean or fully understand what you are saying.

Situations can change quickly from positive to negative. As a foreigner, it is your responsibility not to aggravate the situation. Be passive and conciliatory. If you seem to have offended someone, apologize. Don't physically touch those you are speaking to or act familiar with them. Ask questions to clarify instead of making statements. Humor does not always translate well in different cultural circumstances so avoid it, but goodwill and a generous attitude always help. Be aware that standards of behavior are different than what you may be used to. For example, Chinese people tend to be shy about having their faces photographed. Always attempt to set the person you are speaking with at ease. This is especially true if the person you are speaking with is an officer or authority figure. It is critical that you show respect to police and uniformed persons. Do not assume you can walk somewhere just because there are no signs telling you not to trespass in that area. Also remember that there are military bases in various mountainous regions of China, and will not appear anywhere on your maps. Stick to the main paths. Hikers have sometimes been accosted when straying off the beaten path in the wrong place, and some have been arrested. In order to avoid this happening to you, always be honest, follow directions obediently, and do not attempt to argue.

People who are ethnically Asian, especially Chinese, will face a different set of circumstances than foreigners of other ethnic or racial backgrounds in China. Regardless of your nationality, if you look Chinese, people will treat you as a Chinese person, regardless of your cultural background or linguistic fluency. You will be expected to be aware of and participate in cultural norms of which you may have no knowledge. This presents an especial danger of miscommunication, as people will assume you know and accept things that you may not. In this situation, it benefits the hiker of Asian ancestry to be especially explicit and responsive to the people and situations you encounter.

As a hiker, you may be visiting places in China where few foreigners go, and you may be the first non-Chinese person some people have ever seen. Being stared at and pointed at is a part of the experience, as are persistent and pointed questions about your age, marital status, income, and other topics that would perhaps be considered sensitive in other countries. Do not take this as rudeness. The people you will encounter are part of a different culture, and are not trying to offend you, but instead are merely curious and trying to learn more about you and why you are in their neck of the woods.

Consider yourself to be a guest in China, and act like it. You are an ambassador of your culture, and people will form opinions about where you come from based on your behavior, and vice versa. Many Chinese people you meet will have strong stereotypical ideas about you based on your country, and possibly even your region. For example, Californians are associated with Hollywood, and Texans with cowboys, ideas that of course come from American movies. Again, smile often, and take this as an opportunity to learn. Part of the enjoyment of hiking in another country is getting to meet people from vastly different cultural outlooks, so enjoy it! Even if your Chinese is limited, your goal is still to leave a positive impression.

In conversation, there are some topics that are best to avoid. With the age of the internet, people all over the world are becoming more aware of global news. You may get questions about your government, politics, or foreign affairs. Avoid such questions. Not only may your answers get you into trouble in the conversation, there is a chance that they could have other consequences. Just steer clear of politics as a topic and emphasize that we are all one. If you are communicating online during your time in China, the same holds true. No discussion on WeChat or other platforms about politics, foreign affairs, the situation of various ethnic groups or any similar topic, even in a joke-based way. Just shrug off such topics and redirect the conversation, which most people will be more than happy to do. If you get persistent questions, simply say you don't know much about what they are talking about.

In short, the key to interacting with people in a foreign country is always respect. It is a privilege for you to be in China. You may experience some culture shock, and it is tempting to make snap judgments about people and things based on what you are used to and what you have heard. Not everything you were taught or absorbed before about China is correct. Resist making assumptions about anything. Avoid categorical statements. Ask lots of questions but base them on curiosity rather than preconceived positions. The

Chinese way of doing things may be different, but is not necessarily either right or wrong. If it just that – different. Respect that the people around you have preferences different from yours and may approach situations with a different attitude. Embracing this outlook will greatly impact on your ability to enjoy your time in China.

Safety
In terms of hiking in China, all the standard safety precautions apply. Be adequately clothed for the environment in which you will be traveling, and have the appropriate gear such as shoes, packs, sunglasses, and sunscreen. Have standard first aid equipment such as gauze and Band-Aids in your kit, as you would in Europe, the U.S., or anywhere else. You may not need to carry as much food and water as you would elsewhere, as people and stands selling these items are usually never far from reach. If you can, always travel with someone else. If something goes wrong, you stand a much better chance of solving the problem or getting adequate help than with one person alone.

Many trails in China consist of stone pavers or steps that have been cut into rock, instead or dirt or gravel. When you are hiking, always take care, as water can make such paths slick. In mountainous areas, mudslides are also not uncommon, so always check the weather report before you begin hiking for the day. Signs may be confusing and trails are not always well-marked, so try and get a copy of a map of where you will be hiking before you begin. Hostels and hotels, of course, are usually good about providing this or can direct you to someone who can.

The wildlife in China, in many of the nature parks and

PREPARING TO HIKE

other well-trod locations are used to getting free handouts from tourists, and can be quite aggressive. If you are traveling through an area frequented by tourists and known for monkeys, it is a good idea to purchase a sturdy walking stick to ward off the belligerent beasts. Always take pictures at a safe distance, and never approach large animals. Even small animals may have sharp teeth and carry dangerous diseases, so it is best to keep your interactions with the furry locals to a minimum. You want to make sure that the only souvenir you take away from them is a camera shot, not a bite mark.

Also, don't touch or attempt to pet any dogs you see in villages or out on the roads and paths. They may look cute, but they could bite, and rabies is out there.

If you are in actual, physical trouble, feel free to loudly call for help. Being in a country with so many people provides the advantage that someone will likely be close by who can assist you. If you become sick, lost, or injured, the first step is to find a person to help, something Chinese people are usually quite willing to do. In terms of distress phone lines, the Chinese police number is 110, and they can redirect you to a more appropriate number if necessary. 120 will put you in contact with the first-aid ambulance staff. Both these numbers are free of charge. If you are in an urban area, it is likely that the receiver of the call will speak some English or will be able to pass the phone to someone who can. However, if you are in a rural location, this likelihood diminishes drastically. It may be helpful to ask a Chinese person nearby to contact the police or other emergency number for you. Once you place a call, you should wait in place for help and gesture enthusiastically to emergency workers once they arrive.

As you can likely infer, your mobile phone is your lifeline. It is your map, translator, and method of communication all in one. Wherever you go, bring backup chargers to avoid running out of battery power, and recharge them whenever possible. Purchase a SIM card with enough data to ensure you don't run out. China's cellphone providers are China Mobile, China Unicom, and China Telecom, all of which have decent coverage all over the country, even in the most remote valleys. If you do happen to lose or break your phone, get a replacement as soon as possible. This will help ensure timely assistance is never far from reach. Basic mobile phones in China are really cheap.

Conclusion

The above information is only a brief introduction to hiking in China, but it is a basis for what to expect. The last section of this book contains a survey of the best scenic areas and hikes in China. We hope perusing these trail descriptions will make you eager to set foot in China's great outdoors and get hiking, as well as giving you a wider understanding of all the treasures this unique country has to offer. Have fun reading, and happy trails!

PREPARING TO HIKE

PART III
THE HIKES

THE NORTH

Hiking the Beijing Area

The Great Wall: Gubeikou
Stretching over thousands of miles, the Great Wall is a manmade wonder of almost mythical proportions, although it is actually not a single continuous wall but hundreds of smaller walls scattered over northern and northwestern China, sometimes intersecting, sometimes not. As a device to keep out the barbarians, it was only partially successful – welcome to China! But since at least the late 18th century, it has been an extremely popular destination for people wanting to tangibly experience China's history. Most visitors to the wall today will see the Mutianyu or Badaling sections to the north of Beijing. Gubeikou is less touristed, but no less spectacular, and for outdoor enthusiasts it is one of the best sections to visit to escape the crowds and see the Great Wall in something close to its natural state.

What today is called Gubeikou is actually four sections of the Great Wall that are connected, the two others nearby, stretching between Panlongshan Mountain and Wohushan Mountain, bisected in the middle by a river that runs along the valley floor, on which sits Gubeikou Town. This area of the wall has not been restored since the Ming Dynasty, and for this reason some consider it more authentic than the sections that have been reconstructed in the modern era. Because of its condition, hiking this section of the wall can

THE HIKES

be difficult and somewhat hazardous, so make sure you are in good physical condition and that you take note of the steep slopes and overgrown vegetation.

In total, the Gubeikou Wall stretches about 40 kilometers, and has nearly 200 towers spaced at an average of about 156 meters between them, of various designs. Each tower had two floors and several arched entrances, allowing soldiers to pass through easily and quickly, and between one and six portholes from which projectiles could be fired. The smallest of the towers could accommodate about ten people, and the largest about a hundred.

The first sections of walls were built as long ago at the 7th century B.C., but most of what is known today as the Great Wall, including the sections at Gubeikou, date from the Ming Dynasty from 1368-1644. The Ming was particularly sensitive to the threat from the north. It replaced the Mongols who had subjugated China more than century before, and was in its turn destroyed by another northern invader, the Manchus. The section of the wall at Gubeikou is reinforced with a second layer of bricks over the original, forming a double lining unique to this section. As you hike, you'll be able to see details of this personally.

How to Get There
The Gubeikou Wall is located in the northeast Miyun County, about 120 kilometers northeast of central Beijing. You can reach the village where the trailhead is located by hiring a driver, or by public transportation. In order to reach the wall by bus, take the 980 Express from Beijing to Miyun, then transfer to bus 25. At Gubeikou Town, get off at the Suidaokou stop. Then follow the signs or ask the

locals how to get to the start of the trail. Because of how the wall is arranged, you will have to hike up one section and then back, and then up the other section and back if you want to head back to Beijing directly. The ticket price at the official entrance is RMB 25.

When to Go
The best months to visit are spring and fall — April and May, September and October — because this is when the weather is most temperate. Since some sections of the wall are not maintained, avoid hiking in the rain, when the rocks and bricks can be very slippery.

Trails
The first and shortest section of the wall heads from the river up Wohushan Mountain. Stretching west of Gubeikou town, the Wohushan Wall is 4.8 kilometers in length, a short but steep distance taking 3-4 hours. The name means "crouching tiger mountain," because it looks like two tigers, one on its stomach, the other on its back. The main highlights of this part of the wall are the "Sister Towers," two towers spaced unusually close together near the river. Some say that from a distance, they look like sisters close to the water holding hands. Further along is the Round Stone Tower, so named because of its unusual shape. You might consider hiking this section at dawn or in the evening, as the lighting makes for some spectacular nature photography.

The Panlongshan section is approximately 5 kilometers long, and stretches to the east of Gubeikou town. Notable features of this section include General Tower and 24-Eye Tower. Of all the towers on Gubeikou, General Tower is

THE HIKES

probably the most well-known, placed at the height of Panlongshan from which the wall's defenses could be monitored with clear lines of sight. It has four arrow slots on each of its north and south sides, and three on those facing east and west. The 24-window tower is about the 20th tower on the Panlongshan section of the wall. Only two sides of the tower are still standing, but this tower is the highest, at an elevation at over 400 meters. Historically, the 24-window Tower protected Longyukou pass. It marks the end of the accessible area for tourists today, as beyond it is a military zone where trespassing is not allowed. In total, hiking this section should also take you between 3-4 hours.

The valley across which the Gubeikou wall stretches was critical in ancient times, as it connected the southern and northern areas of the Yanshan Range. Practically, this meant it was the perfect avenue for invaders to access the plan on which Beijing is situated. Through history, more than 130 battles were fought along this area of the wall as the Mongols and other ferocious enemies tried to breach it. This section of wall was a battlefield again even in the 1930s when the Chinese army fought the Japanese invaders nearby. A total of 360 Chinese soldiers died in the battle and are buried in a local cemetery. As you hike the comparatively well-preserved and original brick edifice, you can imagine being a Chinese soldier, looking out into the wilderness beyond the greatest empire in the world.

Fenghuangling 凤凰岭自然风景公园

Due to its scenic natural environment and proximity to the northwest of Beijing, Fenghuangling Nature Park, also known as Phoenix Mountain, is an ideal chance for Beijingers and visiting hikers to get out of the city and enjoy the western hills. The Fenghuangling park covers an area of nearly 18 square kilometers, and this tranquil preserve is a mere 30 kilometers from downtown Beijing. Within the park's perimeters are clear springs, several tiers of forest ecosystems, and rocky cliffs popular with rock climbers. The mountain has sites relating to all three of China's religious and philosophical traditions – Taoism, Buddhism and Confucianism –and there are over forty attractions that hikers can visit by following the three main trail routes. The northern section is better known for its natural features, while the central section, starting at Longquan Temple, is famous for its importance in Chinese traditional medicine.

The ticketed entrance to Fenghuangling is near a Buddhist temple called Longquan Monastery, originally constructed in the Liao Dynasty (907-1125). This temple is known to attract highly-educated monks who are students at China's top universities. In recent years, they have built a 60-centimeter robot based on a cartoon character named Monk Xian'er (贤二机器僧), who has become something of a celebrity. There are statues and images of him scattered around the temple grounds. In addition to their regular duties, the tech-savvy young monks use China's social media like WeChat and Weibo to spread Buddhist principles.

THE HIKES

How to Get There
To get to the park from downtown Beijing, take subway line 4 to Beigongmen, and then bus 346 to the end stop, Fenghuangling. Travel time by public transport – allow 1.5 hours or so. Follow signs from there to the entrance. The ticket price is RMB 25.

When to Go
In March, the peach trees at the base of the mountain are in bloom, especially around the park entrance. Between the bus stop and the ticket office along the main road is a pick-your-own orchard, and from May to October you can sample apricots, peaches, plums, pears, and apples as they successively come into season.

Trails
There are three trail loops, the north, south, and middle trails, with additional side paths to different sites and overlooks. The main trail of the north route is 4.2 kilometers, plus an extra 2 kilometers from the entrance along the middle route. It is the most popular of the three trails, with an abundance of historic sites and scenic overlooks. Some of the highlights included the Geyi Nunnery; Tianti, the so-called ladder that leads to heaven; the Li'er Harbor Coast Cliff, a seacoast landform thousands of years old; and the Immortal's Footprint, a stone tablet with a footprint-shaped impression. Legend tells that the rock fell down the mountain towards a group of children, but an immortal kicked it out of the way, saving the children and leaving his footprint. There are also many springs, grottoes, and pagodas for hikers to enjoy.

The middle route is 2 kilometers long and starts at Langquan Monastery, then winds into the mountains through a series of caves, the Immortals' Cave, Three Buddha Cave, Xuanyuan Cave, and the Immortal's Chair. This complex is historically associated with traditional forms of medicine and health. Further along is the Baita Reservoir and Shade Pavilion where the immortals – older gentlemen with prominent foreheads and flowing white beards – like to play chess. This route also has a cliff inscribed with the characters for Phoenix Mountain, the largest rock inscription in the Beijing area.

The south route is 4.6 kilometers, and is better known for its scenic beauty than its more sparse historic sites. Again starting from Longquan Monastery, hikers can see the Huangpu Courtyard, Guandi Temple, and Luzu Cave, all of which are important to the Buddhist, Taoist, and Confucius traditions. Other special attractions include Jingang Stone Pagoda and the Stone Buddha Sculptures of the Northern Wei Dynasty. This route is less crowded than the other two, and offers some of the best natural vistas.

Mt. Yangtaishan Scenic Area 阳台山 and Jiufeng National Park 鹫峰森林公园

Unlike Fenghuangling, Yangtaishan, the "terraced mountain," has fewer historic sites but is quieter, and has a verdant landscape. Most of the temples were built in the Liao and Jin Dynasties (about 1,000 years ago), and includes one of the Liao's 72 garrison posts. The architecture in the area was developed further during the Ming and Qing dynasties, a few centuries later. The most famous of these is Dajue Temple, located at the foot of Yantaishan Mountain. The temple complex is over 1,000 years old, and is associated with some of China's most famous calligraphers and writers. It is also known for its tall cypress, gingko, and white magnolia trees.

How to Get There
The Yangtaishan Scenic Area is directly south of Fenghuangling, along the same Phoenix Ridge. It is also easily accessible from downtown Beijing, as it is at the end of subway line 16. You can also reach the area by the same bus as Fenghuangling, or you can take no. 633 and walk an extra kilometer to begin at Dajie.

When to Go
This area has similar weather to Fenghuangling. Spring can be a particularly pleasant time to visit, when the flowers are in bloom. Avoid public holidays, as this will make all the nature parks in the Beijing area more crowded.

Trails
The most interesting part of Yantaishan and Jiufeng are the old pilgrimage trails that snake through the hills. One such trail starts at Dajie and makes its way north to Jinshan Temple. The hike is about 5 kilometers long, and will take you past several pavilions and the remains of old teahouses. The temple at the end, Jinshan "Golden Mountain" Temple, is famous as the place where French Nobel laureate in literature Saint-John Perse wrote his principle poetic work, *Anabase* while on assignment as a diplomatic press corps attaché for the French in Beijing during WWI, from 1916-1921. A longer hike heads south over the ridge, ending

at Jiangou Village at the base of Miaofengshan Mountain. This is the traditional pilgrimage route over 10 kilometers long, and scales the ridge, so it will take 3-4 hours.

The Ming Tombs

The Ming Tombs are a popular hiking site, which many people like to combine with a visit to the Badaling section of the Great Wall. However, the tombs are well worth a visit and a hike in their own right and there is more than enough to see to fill several days. Located about 45 kilometers northwest of central Beijing is a valley containing the remains of thirteen of the sixteen Ming Emperors, as well as two princes and upwards of 30 imperial concubines who lived and died between 1409 when the Dynasty was founded to 1644 when it feel to the invading Manchus. The tombs fan out in a meticulously planned system, with each mausoleum its own self-contained area including underground palaces, huge statues of men and animals, and magnificent archways. The location of the tombs was chosen according to the principles *feng-shui*, or Chinese geomacy. Hence, the tombs are surrounded on three sides by mountains, and a river flows nearby. The area was designated a UNESCO Heritage Site in 2003.

How to Get There

The tombs are accessible by bus. From Deshengmen Station, you can take bus 872 to Dingling and Changling Station. From Desheng West Station, you can take bus 345 Express or bus 886, change at Changping Dongguan, and get on bus 314 to Nanxin Village Station. Either route will take you a little over an hour. You can also reach the tombs

THE HIKES

by subway, by taking the Changping Line to Changping Dongguan Station and then transferring to bus 314. Do not get off at the Ming Tombs Station, as it is still 4 kilometers from the scenic area, and hired cars here are expensive.

Trails

Once you arrive in the area of the tombs, the most traditional way to approach the tombs is down the Shen Dao, or "Sacred Way," a 7-kilometer path that begins at the Great Red Gate, a gigantic memorial archway constructed in 1540 that is one of the largest of its kind in China. The Shen Dao ends at the Changling Tomb, the mausoleum of the third emperor. In addition to the mausoleums, hikers will observe the Shengde Stone Memorial Archway, Dragon and Phoenix Gate, the Five-Arch Bridge, and the Stele Pavilion, among other historic structures. But most likely to strike the eye are the giant stone sculptures lining the avenue. There are a total of 36, divided evenly to each side, two thirds of them animals and one third humans. Up to 30 cubic meters each, their dynamic forms were designed to represent the power of the emperors. Each was pushed to its final location in the winter, by pouring water on the road to create a floor of ice. It would still have been a grueling haul for the laborers.

Not all the tombs are open to the public all the time. But all of them are worth strolling past, open or not. But the main ones, most notably the Changling, Dingling and Zhaoling tombs are open to the public pretty much all the time. As you walk along the Shen Dao, you should detour to see the splendid grounds and treasures of at least one of these tombs. Remember when you arrive that you may only have time to see one or two of the tombs, as it is easy to spend an entire day hiking the main path and exploring the extensive grounds of the mausoleums, not to mention the villages and hills around about. And there are other sites in the area worth visiting.

The design structures and layouts of the thirteen tombs are similar, but do vary in terms of the scope and intricacy of their construction. Each is located at the foot of a mountain or hill, facing outwards to the valley. They are separated by anywhere from 500 meters to eight kilometers.

If you only visit one site, try to see the Changling Tomb. This is the burial site of the third Ming Emperor, Zhu Di, who ruled from 1402 to 1422, and his final resting place is the largest of the tombs. Visitors can view the 1,956-square-meter Hall of Eminent Favor under Tianshoushan Mountain, ornamented with thirty-two 12.5 meter high wood columns, each crafted from a single tree trunk, and hauled to the site from as far as 1,000 kilometers away. The tomb is further bedecked with jade exhibits and a towering statute of the Emperor himself, as well as an estimated 3,000 unearthed precious objects. Above ground is the Ling'en Palace, the Blessing and Grace Palace, used for making sacrifices to Emperor Zhu Di and the Empress Xu. This palace is one of the most precious examples of rare wooden architecture remaining from ancient China. Hikers can see an imposing bronze statue of the Emperor sitting on a throne encircled by nine dragons.

Another site you should spend some time exploring is the Dingling Tomb. This "Fixed Tomb" includes stone thrones, twenty-six red caskets, and subterranean palace chambers. Dingling is only the third-largest tomb, but it is arguably the

THE HIKES

most exquisite, though the structures above ground, except for the soul tower, have crumbled. The architecture of the tomb is particularly interesting because it was constructed without beams or columns. In the exhibition hall, visitors can survey a collection of the 3,000 funerary objects unearthed from the tomb, including a gold phoenix crown with the design of two dragons playing with a pearl. This motif is common, and can be seen repeated across a wide range of sculpture and architecture in China.

Besides the tombs and cultural relics, hikers can enjoy the mountain landscape. Not only are the Ming Tombs well-placed as the burial place of the heads of a dynasty, but the beauty and harmony that inspired the tombs' occupants is also attractive to modern-day hikers. If you would like to explore more of the natural scenery around the area, there is a trail less than 10 kilometers in length that starts from the north end of the Changping tomb, near the campus of Zhengfa University, which extends to a reservoir that is passed when walking along the Shen Dao. This trail takes a few hours, and when you finish, you can return by bus to Changping and then take the subway back to central Beijing.

HIKING THE BEIJING AREA

Hiking in Jiangsu

The Nanjing City Wall 南京城墙

Just about all sizeable cities and towns in old China had a city wall with gates that were guarded and closed overnight. They were mostly demolished over the 20th century, and those few that made it through have had trouble surviving the ravages of economic expansion and industrialization. The Nanjing City Wall is a rare exception, with over 21 kilometers of well-preserved wall and 13 gates remaining, with walkways along most of the demolished sections. It is the longest continuous city wall in the world. At one time, four different fortifications encircled Nanjing City, including two around the larger metropolis and two around the Imperial City and the Emperor's Palace, but today only the inner city wall is intact. The wall is a masterpiece of Ming-era architecture, varying in height between 14 and 21 meters and having a width of as much as 14 meters. Its history began in 1366, when the first Emperor of the Ming Dynasty, Zhu Yuanzhang, ordered its construction on the advice of his councilors. The number of workers it took to complete the project is unknown, with estimates ranging from 200,000 to as many as a million, and it was financed by the wealthy families of the Yangtze River valley. Twenty years later in 1386, the wall's full length was completed. Nanjing was the capital not only of the Ming dynasty, but

THE HIKES

also of the Taiping rebels in the 1850s and of the Republic of China between 1927 and the japanese invasion in 1937, so the wall encompasses a lot of history.

How to Get There
You can get to various point of the wall by bus, train, or simply by walking, depending on where you are staying. The ticketed stretches of the wall are well-marked, with descriptive signs and estimates of the distance between landmarks. The hike itself is easy, as you will be walking along the top of a well-maintained stone barricade with an average width of 7 meters and height of 12 meters, but considering its length, walking the full stretch will take an entire day, at least 10 hours. Entrance fees at the gates vary, but are usually RMB 20.

When to Go
The wall can be accessed at all times of the year. As there is no shade up on the wall, you may wish to avoid hot days, especially during the summer. Winter is a particularly interesting time to visit, and snow can make for unique and captivating scenery, but be careful if the masonry is icy.

Trails
If you can only hike part of the wall, try walking the section from Guanghuamen Gate to Zhongyangmen Gate. This is the northeast section of the wall, and will take you past the tomb of the first Ming emperor in Zhongshan Park, Xuanwu Lake, and the Nanjing City Wall Museum. It is a little over 10 kilometers, and should take from 2-3 hours, minus any side excursions. Heading north from Guanghuamen Gate,

hikers will reach Jiefangmen Gate at the midpoint, where you can see Xuanwu Lake to the north, a huge sparkling artificially-enlarged reservoir shrouded in willow trees. To the east, you can see Purple Mountain, whose hills contain the tomb of the first Ming emperor and that of Sun Yat-sen, the first President of the Republic of China who died in 1925. To the south lies a pagoda, Jiming Temple, and to the west is the skyline of downtown Nanjing, now crenellated by skyscrapers. A little farther north of this gate is a small museum that houses some photographs and small exhibits. If you hike north and west, you will reach the next major landmark, Xuanwu Gate. This entrance was added in the Qing era, China's last imperial dynasty, to allow easy passage from the city to the lakeshore. You can end at Zhongyangmen Gate at the northern tip of the reservoir, or turn west.

A particularly special feature of the wall is the cement used in its construction. A mixture of lime, tong oil and a glutinous rice paste, the cement has held 300-350 million bricks together with remarkable durability for nearly 700 years, through multiple eras. Another feature many hikers begin to notice after walking for some time are the stamps in the hand-made bricks, each of which has the mark of its maker. The stamps were required of the brick-makers—if a brick broke or failed in some way due to shoddy workmanship, the fault could be traced back to the craftsman and the official responsible for that section, who would be liable to strict punishment. The stamps are also proof that the bricks matched specific size specifications, the majority weighing about 10 kilograms and 40-50 centimeters in length. As for the inscriptions, they vary from a single character to over seventy, illustrating the development of typography during the Ming period.

The most impressive gate is Zhonghuamen, on the wall's southern section along the Qinhuai River. Dubbed the "Gate of the Nation" by the Nationalist leader Chiang Kai-shek, this gate resembles a fortress more than a gate. The main archway had 1,000-kilogram sliding doors that rose and fell. It consists of a series of courtyards connected by narrow tunnels and guardrooms, overlooked by high walls containing 27 vaults, which were designed to provide cover for dozens of firing positions. Defenders could allow invaders to rush into the courtyards through the bottleneck entrances, and then slaughter them with impunity. This technique was used to great effect with machine guns against the Japanese army in 1937, although the city ultimately fell to the invaders. Like, Jiefangmen Gate, Zhonghuamen Gate has a museum, this one tucked inside the vaults of the old barricades where you can learn about the wall's history and construction. The entrance fee at this gate is RMB 20, and it is near several bus stops. Although this section is shorter than the northeast section, if have time you should attempt to hike part of it, if only so that you can examine the fortress. Sunset along this section is also stunning, and makes for great evening photography.

Hiking in Gansu

The Mogao Caves 莫高窟
The wonders of Mogao Caves are a product of two elements—a convenient natural landscape, and positioning near the confluence of two branches of the Silk Road at a major trading hub, the oasis of Dunhuang in northwest China. During the 3rd century B.C., Dunhuang became a locus of travel and trade, not only material goods but also religious ideas. Monks began to congregate in the area, using the local caves as retreats to meditate. Eventually, they began to enlarge their grottoes by carving away the soft desert rock, creating temples that accumulated offerings from the wealth passing through the region. By the 7th century there were more than 1,000 caves in the Dunhuang area sheltering thousands of splendid statues and paintings. However, in the 10th century trade routes shifted from land to sea, and Dunhuang was depopulated, the monks abandoning their sumptuous caves. They left behind nearly 50,000 objects of priceless historical value, many sealed away in isolated grottos.

In 1900, a Taoist priest named Wang Yuanlu was working to restore and preserve some of the old caves, and stumbled upon a cell that had been sealed off in the 11th century. The cave was stacked floor to ceiling with the area's oldest silk artifacts, preserved by the darkness and the arid atmosphere. Giddy with his find, Wang Yuanlu tried to offer the contents to local officials, but uncomprehending their value, they told him to simply seal the treasures away again. Seven years later, a British-Hungarian adventurer named Aurel Stein was traveling around central Asia and western China and happened to hear about Wang and the treasure he guarded. Stein met with the priest, and slowly worked at convincing him to show the explorer the hidden cave.

Eventually, Wang gave in, and when Stein saw the priceless artifacts he knew he wanted to bring them back to Britain and cement his fame. He bought 24 cases of manuscripts, or around 10,000 documents, and four cases of paintings and relics from Wang for the equivalent of £130, and then promptly sold them all to the British Museum. Other explorers soon followed on his heels, excavating and looting more of the caves Wang had been caring for, and bringing more of the wealth of documents and artifacts contained in the caves to European museums, leaving only the wall paintings and the heavier carvings, which they could not remove. Today, the Mogao Caves site contains 492 caves stretching 24 kilometers, with 45,000 square meters of frescos and more than 2,000 stucco statues. It is one of the most significant Buddhist art complexes in the world. The area was designated a UNESCO World Heritage Site in 1987.

How to Get There
In terms of transit, there are flights into Dunhuang airport, or there are trains. The fastest train connection at the time of writing is about 24 hours from Beijing with a change at

Lanzhou. Once there, a bus system connects Dunhuang city to all the major scenic locations in the area. Your hotel will be able to provide you with a map with the most up-to-date times and routes. The Mogao Caves can be accessed with the city no. 3 bus, which departs approximately every half an hour and will take about an hour from central Dunhuang. Alternatively, you can hire a taxi, which will take about 30 minutes.

The caves are a highly popular destination, and as a result the number of daily visitors has had to be restricted to 6,000 a day. Tickets can be reserved in advance, and definitely should be during the high season (May 1 to October 31). This can be done through the official Mogao Caves website up to thirty days in advance, although an English version of the site is not presently available. The cost is currently RMB 160. After purchasing your tickets, you can collect them at the entrance gate with the ID you used to book them, normally your passport. English language tours are available at 9:00am, 12:00pm, and 2:00pm, at a cost of RMB 180 (RMB 100 in the off season), RMB 80 for students. Fifteen caves are open if you have a regular pass, and closed caves can be viewed for an extra RMB 200 per cave. Plan to spend around two hours on the tour, with a few extra hours for looking around on your own once it has finished. It is highly recommended that you bring your own flashlight, with fresh batteries, as the caves' interiors are dimly lit.

When to Go
Hikers should attempt to avoid the warmer months and instead visit in the spring or fall. In July, temperatures can

THE HIKES

reach as high as 38°C. If you visit, be prepared for desert hiking, and bring plenty of bottled water.

Trails
Once you finish seeing the caves, you can hike around the Mingsha Dunes for a couple hours. The climb to the top of highest peak is 1.7 kilometers, and you will be fighting sand all the way. It is not a walk to be started in the afternoon or in the summer. You can rent a pair of shoe protectors for RMB 15, and should also bring a hat and a scarf to cover your mouth. Since this is the desert, bring water and drink it frequently. At the base of the colossal dunes, you can visit the famous oasis Crescent Moon Lake, which has managed to avoid filling with sand, and in the event you become too exhausted to use your own two feet, you can take a camel ride, and experience how traders on the silk road travelled over the centuries. If possible, try and hike the dunes at dawn or dusk, as the weather will be coolest at these times and you can experience the desert scenery in spectacular lighting.

Zhangye National Geopark 张掖国家地质公园
One of the most unique and picturesque places in China is Zhangye Danxie Landform, Gansu's famous so-called "rainbow mountains." The Danxia Landform was first mapped and named by geographer Fen Jinglan in 1929. The character "Dan" (丹) means vermillion, and "Xia" (霞) means sunglow. Fen named the area after a poem by Caopi (187-226), which begins

HIKING IN GANSU

"The vermilion glow of the sun beneath the clouds
A rainbow hangs from the sky...
丹霞蔽日。采虹垂天..."

The hills of the Danxia Landform are made of multi-colored diagonal stripes, created over millions of years as erosion stripped back the mineral-rich soil. As the sand and mudstone were wore away, chemicals in each layer tinted the dirt a different shade. The result is a spectacular landscape of banded hills, miles of painted rock unobscured by trees or vegetation. The pattern of the bands combined with the shadows from clouds creates a stunning panorama, especially popular with Nature photographers.

How to Get There
Zhangye Geopark is about 40 kilometers from the city of Zhangye, meaning that the north entrance can be reached in 30-45 minutes of driving time, either by bus or in a car. Entrance tickets are RMB 45 for an adult, and an extra RMB 10 to bus to different locations around the park. In the summer, Zhangye is open from 7:00am-6:00pm, and in the winter from 7:30am-5:00pm, with variations depending on the weather conditions.

When to Go
Hikers should consider trying to visit from June to September, as this is when the weather will be most humid and cool. Bring plenty of water, a good hat, and a hiking pole if you need it, as you will be walking in an arid environment. If you enjoy nature photography, this will also be one of your best opportunities in China to take photos.

THE HIKES

Trails

The Danxia Landform has six viewing platforms, connected by buses that provide convenience for tourists. However, you can hike along the road between platforms, about 10 to 15 minutes per segment. The first viewing platform is about a 10-minute hike from the north entrance, and actually consists of several platforms. If you visit all of them, you can spend half an hour to an hour at this point. From there, you can hike to the second viewing area in about ten minutes, although this will be some of the most strenuous hiking as the second platform is the highest in the park. This platform provides 360-degree views, but the climb is 666 steps, or about half an hour to the top. You should be in good physical condition if you decide to climb up to this platform.

At the third viewing platform, you can see the "seven color screen," the steps made of three different colors to complement the surrounding mountains in similar shades. The fourth viewing platform is considered to be the best spot to see the sunrise or sunset, as it sits in a ridge stretching east to west. The alignment with the horizon and the deep shadows in the valleys in this area make it a fantastic location to take pictures during the early and late hours of the day, the reds in the soil making it seem at if the hills are on fire. When ready, you can take the bus back to the entrance.

HIKING IN GANSU

Hiking in Hunan

Wulingyuan 武陵源
The Wulingyuan Scenic Area is actually divided into four areas: Zhangjiajie National Forest Park, Yuanjiajie Scenic Area, Tianzi Mountain Nature Reserve, and Yangjiajie Scenic Area. At around 260 square kilometers, this area near the center of China contains a wide range of natural wonders to explore. The karst landscape is the product of years of erosion, resulting in the dramatic sandstone-quartz pillars covered in lush foliage that were popularized around the world by James Cameron's movie *Avatar*. The UNESCO World Heritage Site has more than 3,000 rock pillars, two natural bridges, and around 40 caves.

How to Get There
Wulingyuan is one of the few destinations in China that is not accessible by high-speed train, only regular train and plane. But this has the advantage that it makes the scenic area less crowded. From the nearest city, Changsha, you can reach Zhangjiajie Town in about six hours by train. From there you can take a bus or taxi to the Wulingyuan entrance from the station in the city center in about an hour.

It is recommended that you stay inside the park if you have a few days, as you then won't have to commute. The town just inside the Wulingyuan entrance is small, but has

THE HIKES

plenty of places to stay and eat. Many visitors recommend staying here over the Forest Park entrance, as there are fewer tourists and there is less distance to the park's highest platform. The entrance fee is RMB 245, RMB 140 for students, but the ticket is valid for four days. The cable cars inside the park cost extra, but the shuttle buses that ferry visitors from one area to another are free. The park is open from 7:00am-7:00pm daily, and the shuttle system runs until the park closes.

When to Go
The rainy season is from April to June, creating mist that may obscure the views and create mudslides, and July through August tends to be quite crowded because of summer vacation. November through March winter will offer some amazing snowy landscapes, but the park may be closed and the trails slippery. The best time of year to visit is between September and October, as the weather is temperate and mist is less likely to obscure the mountain terrain.

Trails
Trails in the park are well-developed and maintained, but may be steep in places given the vertical variation in terrain. Take this and your physical condition into account when you are planning where you want to hike. While not strictly a hiking activity, you may wish to ride the Bailong Elevator. For RMB 72 for a single trip, you can rise 326 meters in a mere 1.5 minutes, which is a Guinness World Record for outdoor elevators. The ride will give you a condensed but breathtaking view of the gigantic karst formations.

The areas around the viewing platforms and the Bailong Elevator are usually crammed with tourists, but the trails are quiet and serene.

One recommended hiking route that takes about a day starts by riding the shuttle from the Wulingyuan entrance to the first cable car up Tianzi Mountain, or hiking approximately 7 kilometers (1,000 stairs) in about 2 hours to the viewing platform at Yunqing rock. At 1,262 meters, this mountain is the tallest in the Wulingyuan Scenic Area and offers incredible views, though you should attempt to visit on a sunny day when the peaks are not shrouded in mist. If you prefer less crowded areas, you can venture a little farther down the road to some scenic spots with fewer tourists. From there, take the shuttle to Enchanting Terrace and walk along the trails back in the direction you came from, towards the Heavenly Pillar and the famous Natural Bridge. This area can be busy, but has some of the most spectacular panoramic views. When ready, take the shuttle to the Bailong Elevator, which you can ride to the valley floor. You can also descend by the trail instead. At the bottom, walk back about 5 kilometers through the valley along the Golden Whip Stream, an easy and peaceful hike.

An alternative route is to take the shuttle to the Bailong Elevator area but have the driver let you off at the start of the trail to the Southern Heavenly Gate. From there, you can hike up to the viewing platforms at the top of the elevator, but be aware that this is some strenuous hiking up around 3,000 stairs and will take you between 2-3 hours. However, it will save you the price of the cable car and time waiting in line.

Hiking in Hubei

Wudangshan Mountain 武当山

Wudangshan's claim to fame is that it is the legendary birthplace of Tai Chi and other Taoist forms of *wushu*, or Chinese martial arts. It was here that the Taoist monks developed their style, a counterpoint to the Shaolin temple school further north. This tradition continues to the present day, and don't be surprised to see students from the surrounding martial arts academies practicing Tai Chi or Kung Fu as you ascend and descend the cliffs. Several popular movies have been filmed at temples on the mountain, including "Crouching Tiger, Hidden Dragon" and the 2010 version of "Karate Kid." The cliffs are honeycombed with Taoist temples and shrines, and with kung fu practitioners. In total, there are 72 temples, 36 Taoist Monasteries, and nine palaces built into Wudangshan's steep slopes and valleys, in addition to hundreds of bridges and thousands of stairs. Of course, over the centuries many of the buildings have burned down or collapsed and have had to be rebuilt. The oldest existing structures are the Golden Hall and the Ancient Bronze Shrine, built in 1307. The climb to the top is strenuous, but full of history and iconic sights.

THE HIKES

How to Get There
Wudangshan Mountain is about equidistant from Beijing and Shanghai, and can be reached from either in about a day by an overnight train. Trains run to Wudangshan Railway Station, which is in a small village about 15 kilometers northwest of the main entrance. You can also fly into Wudangshan Airport halfway between Shiyan City and the scenic area, and then take a bus to the park in under 1.5 hours. Buses run from Shiyan Town to the park as well.

There are accommodation options inside and outside the park. The ones inside are more expensive, however hikers who leave and re-enter the park have to pay RMB 30 per entrance on top of their RMB 140 ticket. For this reason, it may actually be more cost-effective to stay within the park, depending on how long you wish to stay.

When to Go
The weather on Wudangshan Mountain is best in the spring and fall. Remember to bring layers of clothing, as the temperature at the base of the mountain is much warmer than at the top. Unlike other scenic areas where festivals simply overcrowd the park, there are certain celebrations that provide unique opportunities at Wudangshan. In early April and October there are boat races on the nearby Han River. During October, the Wudang International Tourism festival takes place, during which time there are art exhibits and martial arts performances. Although the park will be proportionately more crowded, these events can also make for a special trip.

Trails

There are two main trails in Wudangshan. The shorter one climbs to Five Dragon Temple, the oldest structure on the mountain. If you have limited time and wish to hike the longer trail, you can also visit by taking a bus up from the base of the mountain to where Five Dragon temple is located. Alternatively, if you speak Chinese you can hire a guide to take you through the 12 kilometers of trails leading from Nanyan Palace on the longer trail, but this route is unmarked. The climb to Five Dragon Temple has numerous attractions, and it is well worth taking the path by foot, and at 5.5 kilometers, it should take 2 to 3 hours. The temple was built in the Tang period, 627 A.D. at the command of the Emperor Taizong, and expanded during the Song and Yuan periods about 500 years later. The largest building was completed during the Ming dynasty under the auspices of the Yongle Emperor, who claimed Xuan Wu as his personal guardian.

The other, longer hiking path splits halfway up and heads to different peaks, although both sections eventually join again in a loop. The left hand trail leads to the Golden Summit, and the right hand trail leads to Purple Cloud Temple. If you take the left-hand route, first you will reach Sky Pillar Peak, which is 1,612 meters high. The last leg of this trail section is particularly difficult, as the path both climbs and descends, making the distance appear shorter than it really is. At the peak is the Golden Hall, named because of the central temple constructed entirely of bronze and dedicated to the Ming Emperor. the entrance fee is RMB 20. The trail loops down a cliff to Nanyang Palace, which was originally built as a temple from 1285-1310,

THE HIKES

and contains fine examples of classical architecture.

From Nanyang, the route descends to Purple Cloud Palace, constructed from 1119-1126, where the final scene in the movie "Crouching Tiger, Hidden Dragon" was filmed. The courtyard is used as practice grounds by Wudangshan's Tai Chi school. Entrance to the complex costs RMB 15. Leaving Purple Cloud Palace, the trail descends to Laojun Hall, completing the loop. In total, this trail is 9 kilometers round-trip. The summit can be reached in as little as 3 hours, but hikers tend to enjoy it more by taking their time and visiting the plethora of treasures that the mountain has to offer. The majority of the trail is made of stairs, making the scenic areas welcome spots to recuperate. In order to fully enjoy Wudangshan, plan on talking at least half a day to hike the mountain.

THE SOUTH

Hiking in Guangxi

The Longji Terraced Fields 龙脊梯田景区

The Longji, or Dragon's Back Terraced Rice Fields are one of the best-known images of China's farming country. Over 66 square kilometers of hillside land have been painstakingly carved into fertile strips of farmland that have been cultivated using traditional irrigation techniques for centuries. Construction began during the Yuan Dynasty (1271-1358), and continued well into the early Qing Dynasty in the 17th century, the last of China's imperial lineages. The Longji Terraces are some of the most fantastic scenery in Guangxi, melding mountains, water, and people into a seamless landscape.

How to Get There

Most visitors to the Longji Rice Terraces will depart from Guilin City, about 100 kilometers to the south. You can rent a private car, although it can be somewhat expensive. Often, your hotel can organize this for you, and transportation by this method will take about 2.5 hours. You can also get there using the public bus, which will be significantly cheaper. First you will take a bus from Qintan Bus Station near the center of Guilin to Longsheng Town, and then on to the Longji Terrace area, each leg taking approximately 1.5 hours for a total of three hours. Some recommend you stop

THE HIKES

before Longshang at Heping, where buses also depart for the terraces. Buses run every 15 minutes.

The price of admission is RMB 100, half for students with ID. You will pay at the ticket office near Jinzhu Zhuang Village before continuing up the road. You can find numerous hostels and hotels at Ping'an or Dazhai, depending on where you want to start hiking.

When to Go
There are no bad times of the year to visit Longji. In spring, the terraces have just been planted, and the sculpted pools of water ribbon the hills. In summer, the growing rice plants turn all the hillsides green, although in late summer some of the shape of the terraces can be lost as the stalks grow to half a meter high. In the fall, the hills turn temporarily golden, and can look brown and bare after harvest. Winter can also be an interesting time to visit, as there will be fewer tourists, and if you are lucky, there might even be snow on the terraces. Try not to do the hike on a rainy day if possible, as many of the dirt paths turn to mud, but low clouds and mist can make for some beautiful scenery. June-November tends to be the driest time of year.

Trails
There are several trails around the terraces, and several that can be extended with side trips. One recommended hike goes from Ping'an, to Zhongliu, to Dazhai Village. Head from Ping'an towards Nine Dragons and Five Tigers viewpoint, which has a panoramic view of the fields and the village. From there, it is about two hours to Zhongliu by a dirt road through a valley, and then another two hours to

Dazhai. The trail is well-used and partly paved with stones, and there are several signs marked on stones between Ping'an and Zhongliu Village. But if you happen to get lost it's easy to ask for directions.

As you walk, the trail meanders from platform to platform, allowing you to take in one of the largest mountain cultivation areas of the Guangxi region. The farms in Longji are mostly operated by the Yao and Zhuang ethnic minorities, and the terraces are their traditional method of cultivation, passed down over the centuries. As you hike, you can see the local architecture, multi-storied wooden houses with levels that often expand over the one underneath, almost like a reverse of the terraces. Dazhai Village is the largest of those in the area, and has been around for over 600 years. As you near the town, you will cross a small wooden bridge, and the village is about a quarter of an hour of downhill walking beyond. If you are not quite ready to end your hike, you can take a detour to the Music from Paradise viewpoint, high up on a nearby hill. In total, this hike is 4 to 5 hours in length, depending on the weather conditions.

If you want to spend more time at Longji, you can do the reverse of this route, from Dazhai, to Zhongliu, to Ping'an. After stopping at Ping'an for lunch, continue south past the "Seven Stars Around the Moon" viewpoint on to Longji Zhuang Village, and from there to either Jinjiang (Golden River) Village or Jinzhu (Golden Bamboo) Zhuang Village, both of which are near each other and the same distance. This will add a little over two more hours onto the hike.

THE HIKES

Yangshuo Scenic Area 仰首

The karst mountains of the Guangxi region are among the most recognizable scenery of anywhere in China. The limestone rock has eroded over thousands of years into fantastical shapes, steep cones that either stand alone (*fengcong*) or appear in groups (*fenglin*), which is the most common type in Guangxi. China's karst belt is among the largest and most spectacular in the world. The rock formations rise sharply from flat river valleys in rounded hills, covered in thick, green vegetation. Due to the unique geography, hiking here involves long, gentle walks along the rivers or steep trails that climb in altitude. Guilin and Yangshuo have around them among the most classical of Chinese landscapes, and hiking here is not to be missed.

How to Get There

You can fly into the Guilin Liangjiang airport at Guilin from any of China's major airports and then take a bus or taxi to one of the train stations. Guilin has three train stations, and two of them, Guilin South Train Station and the Yangshuo Train Station, both offer shuttle buses directly to Yangshuo. The ride will take about an hour and a half from each. If you are taking a train to Guilin, you may need to transfer between train stations in order to get a bus to Yangshuo. The nearest major metropolises are Shenzhen and Hong Kong, from which you can reach the city by rail in about three hours. As for accommodation, Yangshuo and nearby towns have many resorts and hotels to choose from.

When to Go

Yangshuo is best visited in spring and late fall, when the days are sunny and the weather is temperate. From March to May and from September through November the temperature is usually below 30°C, or 85°F, and the skies are generally clear. However, in November and December the days, while cool, are rarely cold and hikers have the advantage of far fewer tourists. From May through to August, Yangshuo experiences heavy rains and hot, humid weather, so it is best to try and visit outside of this period. Of course, during holidays this popular destination will be packed.

Trails

One trail you can hike is from Xingping to Daizu Hill. It's about 15 kilometers, but the flat terrain means it will only take between 4 and 5 hours. First, take the ferry across the river. From Xingping village, the hike follows the river east along a stone path for a ways before turning into a dirt road. This section passes through dense bamboo thickets and orchards of orange trees. After about 2.5 kilometers a narrow path branches off and goes up Daizu Hill, which leads past a small monastery. From the top of Daizu Hill, you can view the wide curves of the river. The trail isn't well marked, but as it's oriented along the river, it's easy to find again if you become confused. Eventually, the trail intersects with a farm road and loops back. Bring snacks and water, as there are few tourist stands along this route.

A half-day hike you might want to attempt runs between Yangdi and Xingping. First, take a local bus south from Yangshuo to Yangdixiang. From there, follow the trail south

THE HIKES

along the Li River. One advantage of this trail is that it lets you enjoy the karst mountains and the river in relative peace, and there are fewer tourists. The trail winds south for a leisurely 18 kilometers, passing through small villages, rice paddies, and bamboo forests. Near Lengshui Village you will be able to see the formation called "Nine Horse Mural Hill." The trail crosses the river three times, where you will have to pay a fee, but the price is only about RMB 16. Along the river you will see small boats and motorized bamboo rafts, which can take you near Xingping if you get tired. Near Xingping you can see the aptly named 20 Yuan-bill Hill, which is the famous ridge printed on the back of the Chinese RMB 20 note. However, while this trail is long, it is quite flat, meaning it should only take 5-6 hours to complete. From Xingping, it is easy to catch a bus back to Yangshuo.

A classic, shorter hike heads up Moon Hill. First reach Moon Hill Village, a 20 minute drive south from Yangshuo. From the town, cross the main highway and follow the signs to the entrance to scenic area, where the ticket gate will charge you RMB 10. From there, climb 700 stone steps to the arch. The mountain itself appears almost perfectly triangular, with a perfect moon-shaped hole seemingly cut from the rock, 50 meters high and across. The trail continues through this arch to the other side of the mountain and then up to its summit. The stone steps are very slippery after rain, so exercise caution and have good shoes. The whole trail to the top and then back to the village will take 2 to 2.5 hours.

If you are looking for a more strenuous hike up the mountains, you might want to hike Wanggong Mountain. Starting from Moon Hill Village, take the country road to the

Jingbao River, about 1.5 kilometers, or 20 minutes. Cross the concrete dam across the river and follow the trail right, back towards where the Jingbao joins the Yulong (Dragon) River. As you walk, you will be able to see a 30-meter high karst that appears rust-colored, called Copper Gate Mountain, with a small cave at its foot. Continue towards the Yulong River and the Yangshuo Mountain Retreat, which should be visible. When you reach the Yulong, you can remove your shoes and cross if the water is less than a half-meter in depth, but if it is high you can ask a local operating a raft to take you across. You can haggle them down to about RMB 10 for the ride. From there, walk back along the road towards the main highway, where you can catch a ride. The entire hike is less than 5 kilometers, and will take 2 to 3 hours. If you want to continue hiking, about half a kilometer from the resort is a graveyard with steps up the hill. There are a series of footpaths beyond that meander through fields to the main highway near Butterfly Cave, where you can take a bus back to Yangshuo.

Hiking in Guizhou

Huangguoshu 黄果树
Huangguoshu Waterfall is the Niagara falls of China, but bigger. During the Ming Dynasty, around 500 years ago, China's great geographer and geologist Xu Xiake once described it in his travel journal like this:

> "The sprays burst apart like pearls and jades and the foams rise like a mist. The waterfall has such momentum that even the couplet 'a screen of pearl released from hooks/or silk that hangs on faraway peaks' cannot fully describe its majesty. I have seen waterfalls that are much higher and more precipitous, but never a waterfall with such a width and magnificence."

At 78 meters tall and 101 meters wide, the falls are the largest in Asia. They are a small part of a geological wonderscape, a 450-square kilometer complex of water and hollow rock rising between the Sichuan Basin and the Guangxi hills. It was re-discovered in terms of the outside world only in the 1980's, when engineers were scouting the area to evaluate how much hydroelectric power it could generate. Today, the flow of the Baishu River is controlled, peaking at about 290 cubic meters per second. Hikers will

THE HIKES

hear the falls long before they see them.

How to Get There
The closest major city to Huangguoshu is Anshun City, 54 kilometers away. There is a minor airport at Anshun, or visitors can fly into the provincial capital, Guiyang, and then take the train as well. From Anshun it's an hour's drive to Huangguoshu Park, or you can take one of the buses to the area that departs from Anshun South Passenger Transport Bus Station. You can also take a bus from Guiyang's Jinyang Passenger Transport Bus Station, but this will take a minimum of 2 hours and may take longer depending on the traffic. There are a variety of accommodation options right outside of Huangguoshu Park, some of which even have a view of the falls. The scenic area is open from 7:00am to 7:00pm, March through November, and 7:30am to 7:00pm from December through February. The price of admission is RMB 180 from March through October, and drops to RMB 160 November through February.

When to Go
Because the size of the park is not as large as some other scenic areas and because it is heavily touristed, it is highly recommended that hikers visit on a weekday during the off-season and avoid public holidays. Unlike some of the bigger preserves where a few minutes walking away from the main scenic locations will significantly reduce the number of people around, in Huangguoshu, it is more difficult to do here. May is a particularly good time to visit, because the river is full but the summer crowds have not yet arrived in force.

Trails

From the parking lot, head up the road northeast and then hook around to the first major scenic area, about half a kilometer along. This site is called the "Garden of Fine Art," and a number of bonsai trees, trained flowers, and statues are on display. Once you have finished with this area, head north along Xuanyuan Rd, passing lotus ponds on the left. The trail slopes gently down past several smaller waterfalls, until you come to the first major overlook for the main falls of Huangguoshu. This fall is unique, as it is the only one you can view from all directions, including behind the waterfall itself, as there are a series of caves behind the falls that you can walk through. There are multiple small paths in the area, allowing visitors to view the water from many angles.

Walk back along the river to the bridge, and then cross and continue to enjoy the view of the falls. From there, walk up the slope to the road that curves around the east side of the park, then take the path to Water Curtain Cave. This cave is a series of natural rooms and windows running a total length of 134 meters behind the water curtain of the falls. From this location, the roar of the water is incredible, as are the rainbows in the mist. When ready, return to the parking lot along the route you came. In total this path is about 5 kilometers, and will take 2-3 hours depending on the crowds.

While you are in the area, consider checking out some of the other sites. Besides Huangguoshu Waterfall, the region is packed with water features and caves because of the geology. About 6 kilometers downstream is the Tianxing Qiao Scenic Area, which has the Tianxing "potted" caves and stone pillars which rise from pools of water. Also nearby

THE HIKES

are the Longgong Caves and the Zhijin Caves, both well worth a visit. The local villages are populated by China's non-Han minorities the Buyi and Miao, and visiting them is a good way to learn about the local culture.

HIKING IN GUIZHOU

Hiking in Chongqing

The Three Gorges of the Yangtze River 三峡
The Three Gorges range along the central reaches of the Yangtze River, one of the most important waterways in China. The river falls down a long step, from the Sichuan plateau down to the central China plain and the deep ravines through which it passes have for many centuries been from praised for their wild and noble beauty and feared for the danger of navigating the many rapids on the course from Wanzhou down to the city of Yichang, below the last gorge. Today the gorges have become a lake thanks to the construction of the Three Gorges dam, to the west of Yichang, which is the largest dam in the world in terms of installed power generation capacity. The dam raised the surface of the water up 180 meters, nearly 600 feet, from the lowest point, and that submerged countless towns and villages, pagodas and temples, and more than a few eminently hike-able paths and trails. But there is still an enormous amount of wonderful country to see, and there are many fascinating hikes in this fascinating mountain region. George Morrison, mentioned above, described the gorges during his travels:

> "Two stupendous walls of rock, almost perpendicular, as bold and rugged as the

Mediterranean side of the Rock of Gibraltar seem folded one behind the other across the river. Savage cliffs are these, where not a tree and scarcely a blade of grass can grow, and where the stream, which is rather heard than seen, seems to be fretting in vain efforts to escape from its dark and gloomy prison. In the gorge itself the current was restrained, and boats could cross from bank to bank without difficulty. It was an eerie feeling to glide over the sunless water shut in by the stupendous sidewalls of rock. At a sandy spit to the west of the gorge we landed and put things in order. And here I stood and watched the junks disappear down the river one after the other, and I saw the truth of what Hosie had written that, as their masts are always unshipped in the down passage, the junks seem to be "passing with their human freight into eternity."

The gorges were formed mostly not by water action, but by the process known as orogeny, when mountains are formed at the collision point between two tectonic plates. This all happened about 70 million years ago, and as the crust rose, erosion intensified, the hard limestone broke and collapsed into vertical fissures, creating steep mountains and deep gorges. Along other parts of the river, softer beds of shale and sandstone create gentler slopes and a wider river.

How to Get There

The Three Gorges Scenic Area starts approximately 30 kilometers west of Yichang. You can take the special bus line from Wuyi Square to the terminal stop near the Xiling Gorge, which takes about 1.5 hours. Multiple buses also travel to the other gorges and towns along the way, so the time and number will vary depending on where you want to hike.

When to Go

The best time to visit is from April to October, when the Yangtze River is full. Also, the mountainous paths can be somewhat difficult to hike during winter when the rocks are icy, and the vegetation won't yet be in bloom.

Trails

One of the best hikes is in Wu Gorge and is called the Goddess Peak Trail. The path begins near Qingshi Town and climbs up to the peak, at an elevation of about 1,000 meters above sea level. On the trail you will walk past Scissors Peak and Songluan Peak, and can watch the many boats on the river below passing along the Yangtze. The hike also has a good view of Goddess Rock, for which the peak is named. According to legend, the rock is the embodiment of a fairy that assisted Yu the Great, who supposedly tamed the great floodwaters of the river. The fairy, Yao Ji, was the youngest daughter of the Heavenly Mother. Along with her eleven sisters, she met Yu at Wu Gorge, struggling to control the habitual floods that tormented the region. Moved to help him, Yao Ji sent Yu a sealed book with instructions on how to control the waters. However, in the process of

THE HIKES

translating the book, she and her sisters were captured by heavenly soldiers. Undeterred, they broke free and returned to Earth where they helped Yu tame the floods. To this day, Yao Ji stands watch over the sailing boats traveling through the gorge. The Goddess Peak hike, up and back, should take about 7 hours at approximately 3 kilometers one-way, so plan to spend a full day on this one.

Xiling Gorge, the longest and deepest of the three, is actually a series of gorges. Before the construction of the Three Gorges Dam, Xiling was known as the most dangerous, with fractious waters and strong rapids. At the reservoir behind the dam, , the water is over 100 meters deep. The dam is the largest hydropower project in the world. Many trails exist in the hills around the reservoir, providing scenic views of the lake and the cliffs. One such trail is the road from Nantuo to Sandouping, which follows along beside the river for 9 kilometers and will take about 2 hours. Though narrow, the trail has fantastic views from within the gorge.

The third and most famous gorge is Qutang. At its western entrance is the so-called Kuimen Gate, one of the most iconic landmarks on the Yangtze River. At its narrowest point, Chijia and Baiyan Mountains squeeze the river to less than 50 meters, while cliffs of over 350 meters rise on either side. This is the image printed on China's RMB 10 banknote. The shortest gorge, Qutang is nonetheless the steepest and considered by many the most stunning, with high vertical cliffs cloaked in mist and lush vegetation. Hiking here is more limited, ands the walls of the gorge are of course 100 meters or so less imposing than they were before the reservoir filled up. But if you can you take a boat ride along the river-lake to enjoy the Three Gorges fully, you will still be overawed.

Hiking in Hong Kong

Victoria Peak and the MacLehose Trail
Hong Kong is one of the most densely populated places on Earth, but perhaps surprisingly, three-quarters of the territory is actually green space, with country parks accounting for forty percent of the preserved area. Hong Kongers take their environment seriously, and as a result there are crystal beaches, lush mountains, and miles of coastline all a short trip from the urban areas, sometimes just a ridge away from extreme urban-ness.

How to Get There
Hong Kong can be reached by train or by plane from all major Chinese and international cities.

When to Go
Hiking in Hong Kong is a year-round affair. In the summer, however, due to the generally tropical climate, hiking can be depressingly hot, so bring proper equipment and plenty of water on the trail. Monsoons are a serious threat in the later summer , and if one is around, don't go hiking. From October through to April the temperatures are the most mild, and hikers are least likely to be inconvenienced by monsoon winds and rains.

THE HIKES

Trails

There are some wonderful walks on Hong Kong island, just above the city madness, visible and audible below you, and the top choice is a walk around Victoria Peak. To get there, take bus 15C from Central Pier 8, bus 15 from Exchange Square, or minibus 1 from MTR Hong Kong Station. The hike consists of a loop made up of Lugard Road and Harlech Road, and begins at the Peak Tower. Lugard Road was built in 1913-1914, and is named after Hong Kong's 14th governor, Sir Frederick Lugard. Walk to the left and you will soon hit plank paths following the steep hillside. In about 20 minutes, you will reach Lugard Road lookout, which has incredible views of Victoria Harbour and is close to the highest point on Hong Kong Island. Eventually Lugard runs into Harlech Road, which circles back towards the starting point along a shaded walkway lined with large trees. Take a moment to stop at Mount Austin Playground and enjoy the waterfall on the south side. The total distance in 3.5 kilometers, and takes about 1.5 hours to complete. Popular times of day to take this hike are at dawn and in the evening, because of the fantastic light. There are a number extended walks to take from this circle. You can turn onto Hatton Road at the intersection of Lugard and Harlech, and head towards Pinewood Battery and take a walk around the campus of the University of Hong Kong. Or you can walk down to the Pokfulam reservoir. To return from the circle walk you can take the bus, or the Peak Tram down to the Garden Road Terminus. Pro tip — start the walking by going to your right as you look out at the city, means the spectacular views of the city come last.

Another idea is to walk from the middle of Central District

straight up the peak. There are a number of routes, but the most direct is via Hong Kong Park and Old Peak Road. It will take an hour or more, depending on how fit you are, and how often you stop, but once you pass the apartment blocks at the top of Old Peak Road, you are suddenly in a forest. It is the most unexpected of transitions.

There are other trails on Hong Kong island, but the MacLehose Trail in the New Territories, north across the harbour and close to the border with Shenzhen, is arguably Hong Kong's most famous hiking path. The MacLehose Trail in its entirety is much longer, stretching 100 kilometers through 8 country parks. It extends from the Sai Kung Peninsular in the east through Kowloon and into the western New Territories. Many Hong Kongers who love the outdoors make it a goal to hike the entire trail. The trail is split up into eight sections, each with its own attractions. A good day trip along stages 2 and 3 winds along the coast, but also heads up into the mountains, and can be accomplished in one day.

Stage 2 begins at Long Ke Beach, a popular swimming and picnic spot. The sand is clean and the water clear, cradled by cliffs of volcanic rock, formed into unique hexagonal columns. After leaving the beach, the trail climbs 300 meters in a short stretch, with little shade. The trail becomes slightly less strenuous after cresting the first peak, continuing to climb along the ridge with spectacular views of the ocean. Eventually the trail curves back down to the water along Sai Wan and Ham Tin beaches, which are popular camping spots. The total distance of this stage is 13.5 kilometers.

Stage 3 begins at Pak Tam Au, and is one of the more

THE HIKES

difficult sections, partly because of a grueling start up stairs to the highest peak so far, at an elevation of 428 meters. The best viewing point is actually three quarters of the way up, and has panoramic lines of sight of the mountains and the ocean. The trail continues to climb up and down along the ridge, through bamboo groves and grassy bluffs. A steep climb over Rooster Hill marks the final stretch of this trail, before the path veers downhill to the beginning of stage 4. Here there is a large campground with excellent facilities, and also a bus stop on Taisha Road that will take you back to the city. Stage 3 has a total distance of 10.2 kilometers.

HIKING IN HONG KONG

THE WEST

Hiking in Sichuan

Emei Mountain 峨嵋山

Mount Emei is arguably the most famous peak in central China, and it has been a holy Buddhist pilgrimage destination for a thousand years. It lies beside Emeishan City, approximately 30 kilometers from Leshan City and 150 kilometers from the provincial capital of Chengdu. The mountain is a UNESCO world heritage site, and was one of China's first National Parks. The name means something like 'eyebrows', in honor of certain peaks that look like the delicate arch of an eyebrow, and Emei is seen by Chinese Buddhists as being the place of enlightenment of the Bodhisattva Samantabhadra, known in Chinese as Puxian, the patron saint of action. Emei was also the site of the first Buddhist temple in the 1st century A.D. By the 3rd century, many of the original Taoist shrines were converted for Buddhist practice, and Emei became one of China's Four Sacred Buddhist Mountains. Given its location in the cultural hub that was Sichuan Province for many Chinese dynasties, Emei became a popular destination for monks and literati alike. In his poem "Climbing Mt. Emei," the 8th century poet Li Bai says:

> So many immortal mountains in Sichuan
> None to compare with Emei,

THE HIKES

> Ascend in circles for the views,
> Unique, strange and peaceful,
> Dark and profound it leans against the open sky
> Color change, a new painting at each turn...
> The mists support me
> Piled-up worldly concerns can be discarded.
> If I meet with the immortals
> Let them take me by the hand as we approach
> the the sun.

Situated at the edge of the Tibetan plateau, Mt. Emei is easily the tallest of China's four sacred Buddhist mountains, at over 3,000 meters above sea level. Dozens of pavilions and monasteries are nestled in the mountain's cliffs and folds. There are four main scenic areas—Baoguo Temple, Qingyin Pavilion, Wannian Temple, and the Golden Summit at the very top. Take your time as you make your way up to properly explore the temple halls and view their many treasures, such as the porcelain Avalokitesvara Buddha and the Depository of Scriptures at Xixiang Chi.

How to Get There
From Chengdu, you can take the inter-city high-speed train to the Emeishan Railway Station in about 1.5 hours. The current entrance fee is RMB 120, or half price with a student ID. Boots with studs are available to rent if you visit in the winter, which is a viable choice because of Sichuan's mild climate.

When to Go
Try to visit in spring or autumn, when the weather will be driest and there are fewer tourists. Be aware that some paths

are more difficult than others, and weather conditions on the Emei region can change quickly. Be cautious of slick rocks and mud from mist and rainfall, as well as the monkeys who are accustomed to stealing food from travelers.

Trails

There are several routes to the top, crisscrossing through steep rocky hills. You can reach the summit in a day, but it is recommended you take an extra day or two to fully explore the available trails. If you have the time, it is especially recommended that visitors stay a night at the summit at Jingding Hotel, which is about 100 USD a night, so you can witness dawn over the mountain's famous cloud cover. Lucky travelers might even see a rainbow halo around the giant Puxian Stupa, the highest golden Buddha in the world.

If you only have a day to spend at Emei, then two recommended sections to hike are from Qingyinge Pavilion to Wannian Temple, near the base of the mountain, and Leidongping to the Golden Summit, which is at the top. The first section is about 3.5 kilometers and should take between 1 and 2 hours, while the second is 7.5 kilometers and should take about 2-4 hours to hike. You can travel from Wannian to Leidongping by eco-bus in about one hour. These two routes will let you see the base and peak of the mountain, as well as some of Emei's most famous temples and their treasures. Of course, if you have more than one day to explore, you can take the time to hike from the base of the mountain to the top, and find accommodation at both the Golden Summit and Baoguo Temple areas.

While near Emei, hikers might want to visit the Leshan Buddha, carved into a cliff face at the confluence of two rivers in the scenic area. The edifice actually depicts Maitreya, the plump, jovial Bodhisattva who is associated with bright happiness. At over 71 meters, the statue was carved by a devout monk who thought the presence of the Buddha would calm the turbulent waters.

The area immediately around the *Da Fo* can be quite crowded. If you would like to climb up the Buddha, arrive early, as the entrance lines tend to be quite long. You can purchase a ticket to the entire scenic area, including many gardens, temples, grottoes, and other attractions for just RMB 70. Depending on your fitness level and the crowds, it may take you an hour to climb to the top of the Leshan Buddha. From there, it's about 40 minutes through an old fishing village and across an ancient bridge to reach Wuyou Temple, which is a serene resting place after the crowds around the Buddha. Upon leaving the scenic area you can either take the bus back to Chengdu, or stroll along the road to the old walled town of Leshan.

Jiuzhaigou 九寨沟风景名胜区

Jiuzhaigou is a vast nature reserve in the Min Mountains in the north of Sichuan, on the eastern edge of the Tibetan Plateau. Deep in the mountains, Jiuzhaigou has so far largely escaped the ravages of Maoism, modernization and industrialization that the rest of the country, although in the 1970s there was extensive logging, thankfully banned in 1979. Since then, the Chinese government has banned deforestation and taken measures to protect the pristine environment and primeval forests of the region. In 1992, the park became a UNESCO World Heritage Site and, in 1997, a World Biosphere Reserve. The reserve is home to a number of endangered species, including the Giant Panda and the Golden Snub-Nosed Monkey, as well as a rodent referred to (elsewhere) as the Duke of Bedford's vole, a creature that survives in only three areas in China's mountainous southern regions. The park is also home to 223 species of birds, including the rare black-neck crane and red-belly golden pheasant. Given its size and variation in altitude, the park has one of the most diverse and rich ecosystems in the whole of China.

Jiuzhaigou is over 720 square kilometers and is comprised of three valleys shaped in a Y formation. Jiuzhaigou literally means "nine village valley," a reference to the nine Tibetan villages throughout the park, seven of which are still inhabited. Legend holds that the spectacular natural scenery was created when the Tibetan goddess Wunosemo was frightened by an envious devil, causing her to drop a magic mirror gifted to her from her lover, the war god Dage. The mirror fell to Earth and shattered, resulting in the 114 glittering lakes scattered across the mountains. More scientifically, the valley's topography is made up of karsts shaped by glacial and tectonic forces. Its previously remote location has protected virgin mixed forests that blanket the terrain from the subtropical valley floor to the chilly highlands. The water is stunningly pristine. Hikers not only can see the reflection of snow-capped mountains on the lakes, but also fallen tree trunks crisscrossing their bottoms.

How to Get There
From Chengdu, you can fly to Jiuzhaigou Airport in about an hour and then take a shuttle to Jiuzhaigou Valley, which also takes about an hour. You can also take a bus, for which

THE HIKES

your tickets should be purchased at least a day in advance. The bus route will take between 7 and 9 hours, depending on the conditions. Accommodations in the area within walking distance of the Park entrance are readily available at a range of prices, from hostels to hotels. Currently, admission to Jiuzhaigou for adults is RMB 190 in the peak season (May 1–Nov. 15), and RMB 80 in the off-season (Nov. 16–April 30). In the peak season the park is open 7:00am-7:00pm, and in the off-season 8:00am-6:00pm. There is a transit system of shuttle buses within the park that carry visitors between the major scenic locations, which will shut down by closing time, so be careful not to miss the last bus if you don't plan on hiking out on foot. Food stands in Jiuzhaigou are surprisingly sparse, so it is recommended to bring your own food. However, while you are visiting the area you should definitely enjoy a cup of local highland barley tea and yak butter tea.

When to Go
The park is open year-round. Consider visiting in the off-season, to avoid the surge of tourists from nearby Chengdu during holiday periods. During the winter, some trails might be closed, especially those in Zechawa Valley, which are at the highest altitude. Check the park website for information, and plan accordingly. In 2017, the park was hit by a 6.9 magnitude earthquake, which caused extensive damage to the trails and facilities. The main sites and trails of the reserve were opened again in March of 2018, but factor this into your plans and do some preparatory research before you visit, and be aware you may need to acquire an entrance ticket through a tour agency.

Trails

Jiuzhaigou's trail system has three main branches that follow the three main valleys, with the Park entrance at the start of the trail in Shuzheng Valley. Most tourists will bus to the first photo spot straight from the entrance, at the juncture of the Y. If you would like to escape the crowds, one way to do so is to hike the first 14 kilometers up Shuzheng Valley to this juncture, a smooth hike on boardwalks that follows the river. As this walk is neither strenuous nor at altitude, it is an easy and pleasant way to see an area of the park that most tourists will miss.

Once you reach the spectacular Nuorilang Waterfall, you have two choices—you can hike up Rize Valley, or Zechawa Valley. Rize has a plethora of lakes and streams, but Zechawa has the highest alpine lake of all. To take full advantage of both routes, you will need to spend at least two days hiking around the park. Instead of beginning from the juncture point, consider busing to the top of each valley and hiking down, skipping the popular and therefore crowded sections of trail, usually the parts with boardwalk, by taking the bus to the next checkpoint. At Rize, starting at the top of the valley means beginning at the Jianyan Platform, and at Zechawa, Changhaizi Lake. Both routes are about 18-kilometers long, but Rize valley begins at a higher altitude. Take this into consideration when planning how long these paths will take you.

A fourth and much less well-known branch of Jiuzhaigou is Zharu valley, which extends southeast from the main Shuzheng gully. This valley, running from the Zharu monastery to the Red, Black, and Daling Lakes, has more of a folk cultural presence than the other three, as the Benbo

THE HIKES

sect of Tibetan Buddhists travel through the Zharu Packway on a traditional route. A group that caters to hikers looking to go off the beaten track, Eco-Tourism Jiuzhaigou, offers a number of guided hikes in this valley, for those who want to get away from paved roads and into a more remote section of the Park. Besides a greater degree of tranquility, Zharu offers the chance to see rare wildlife, sacred natural wonders, a shrine to Zhayizhaga, the holy mountain, hideouts dating from China's civil war in the 1940s, and Jiuzhaigou's two abandoned villages. For more information about hiking in Zharu, you can visit the park website.

Hiking in Yunnan

Tiger Leaping Gorge 虎跳峡
Tiger Leaping Gorge is the jewel in Yunnan's crown, one of the most celebrated hiking destinations in China. The origin of the name is debated and myths and legends abound, one of the more popular being that a tiger leapt the gorge at its narrowest point in order to avoid hunters. The exact point, of course, is widely contested among the locals. Most likely, the Gorge took its name from any number of rock formations in the middle of the river that resemble a tiger leaping, although many guesthouses claim that the formation nearest them is the true inspiration and encourage hikers to go down to the river and see for themselves.

The mountains of Yunnan on the east edge of the Tibetan Plateau are the product of millions of years of tectonic grinding, pushing Himalayan rock up towards the sky. Three of China's largest rivers have their headwaters here—the Yangtze, Lancang, and Nujiang. One twelfth of the world's entire population lives in the catchment areas of these different rivers, the upper reaches of which are divided by 6,000-meter ranges of sandstone and limestone. Tiger Leaping Gorge was formed by the Jinsha River, which forms the raging headwaters of the Yangtze. On either side are the ranges of Jade Dragon and Haba Snow Mountains, which soar more than 5,000 meters above sea level. The

THE HIKES

sheer cliffs of the mountains give the gorge its spectacular shape and its reputation as the deepest in the world. Unlike other Himalayan hiking areas such as those in Nepal and India, the gorge can be accessed year-round.

The ethnic group that live in the gorge are predominantly the Naxi people, who are believed to have migrated from the northern Tibetan Plateau centuries ago. They have a distinct culture, practicing a religion based on folk traditions instead of Buddhism or Taoism, and their language has two distinct hieroglyphic scripts, Dongba and Geba. When walking through the gorge, you may see traditional Naxi architecture, which usually consists of two-storey log cabins constructed without nails, with a courtyard in the middle. The doors are typically elaborately designed, carved and painted with plants and animals. Many of the guesthouses you see along the trail will be in this style.

How to Get There
Tiger Leaping Gorge owes at least part of its popularity to how accessible it is—most of the trailheads can be reached by car or bus a mere two hours from Sanyi International Airport near the city of Lijiang. The bus route from Lijiang to Baishutai goes through the Gorge, so you can get off at the main trailhead or at some point along the lower road if you prefer. The main trailhead can be reached from the town known locally as Qiaotou, and in English officially as Tiger Leaping Gorge Town. The entrance fee should be RMB 65, and you should keep your ticket stub to avoid the risk of being charged twice, as it is valid for the duration of your time in the gorge area. If you do not intend to spend more than a day, you can leave your heavier pack at either Tiger

Leaping Gorge Yixiang Hotel or Jane's Tibetan Guesthouse, both of which provide luggage storage for a small fee.

When to Go
The best times to visit Tiger Leaping Gorge are April through May and September to October, which are the driest seasons. Be wary of visiting during monsoon weather from June through August, as the dirt trails can turn to rivers of mud, and landslides are common.

Trails
Hiking Tiger Leaping Gorge presents two main hiking options, the upper trail and the lower trail. The upper route is the actual trail, and the lower path down to the river is a more leisurely walking option. Typically, visitors can complete the upper trekking route from Qiaotou to Walnut Grove in between one long day and three. If you have the time before starting the main trail, 4 kilometers along the lower road from town there is a series of boardwalks leading directly to the river.

Beginning at the Qiaotou trailhead, the trail is a steep climb, winding its way through Naxi alpine villages. In a few hours, you can hike 5 kilometers to reach the Naxi Family Guesthouse, which has stunning views and offers some of the best quality accommodation in the gorge. Immediately after, is the infamous "28 Bends" section, a series of seemingly never-ending switchbacks which nevertheless provide some of the best views. It is here that the trail reaches its highest point, at about 2,650 meters above sea level, up from a starting point of about 1,850 meters. This part of the path is not easy, but can be hiked

THE HIKES

by anyone in a reasonably fit condition if they are willing to climb numerous stairs.

At the top of the "28 Bends" is Yongsheng Village, 5 kilometers from the Naxi Guesthouse, where hikers can rest at the Tea Horse Guesthouse. Nearby is also the Halfway Lodge, which claims the distinction of allegedly having the toilet with the best view in the world. If you reach this point by noon, you should be able to hike 7 kilometers to where the trail joins the main road by mid-afternoon, at Middle Tiger Leaping Gorge. One of the more popular places to stay or eat here is Tina's Guest House. If you continue down the main road for about an hour you will eventually reach Walnut Grove, where you can rest at the Tibet Guest House, Sean's Guest House, or Chateau de Woody. If you still have some time, there is a trail at Walnut Grove called the "Ray of Sunshine Trail," which can take half a day to a day to hike. When you are finished you can take the bus or hire a car from Walnut Grove back to Lijiang.

Shilin National Scenic Area (The Stone Forest)
昆明市石林风景区

Shilin Stone Forest, also called Kunming Stone Forest, is a world of fascinating geologic formations. Like many other places in China's southern regions, the stone forest is a karst landscape created by the erosion of limestone. In the Shilin area, the rock is shaped into karst pinnacles—straight, vertical spires resembling petrified wood, which gives the area its name. Folktales about these mysterious rocks abound, particularly in the traditions of the Sani, a branch of the Yi, a local ethnic minority. Shilin is also close to the provincial capital, Kunming, which was one of the principal junctures of the southwest Silk Road, from which two branch routes extended into present day Burma (Myanmar) and Vietnam. As a result, the area is tied to the history of both China and Southeast Asia, and has a long history of travel and trade.

How to Get There
Buses leave regularly from Kunming Airport and from Kunming East Coach Station for Shilin, and take a little over 1.5 hours. You can also take a train from Kunming South Railway Station to Shilin West Station, about 20 minutes. Buses leave from Shilin Village to the scenic area at intervals of every half-hour, and the trip takes about 40 minutes. There are plenty of accommodations at a range of prices in both Kunming and Shilin.

When to Visit
Perhaps surprisingly, winter is actually one of the better times to visit the Stone Forest. November through April are some of the drier months, and the subtropical climate means the region doesn't get cold in the winter. In the other half of the year, the area tends to experience torrential rains, which can make hiking less pleasant. Additionally, there are fewer tourists than in the summer, which can be an advantage when visiting China's more popular sites, such as this one.

Trails
The widest loop around the scenic area totals about 5 kilometers, and takes about an hour to hike straight through. Start from the entrance across Shilin Lake, and then head right towards the Major Stone Forest and Jianfeng Pool. This

THE HIKES

will take you past the stone stuck between two rock peaks. The trail curls around Jianfeng Pool before joining a loop that contains Wangfeng Pavilion and the formation called "A Phoenix Combing Her Feathers." Exit the loop onto the trail that heads towards the "Mother and Son" formation. The path then curves back towards the Bushaoshan Scenic Area. This area has many marine fossils, most from the Permian Period around 290 million years ago. From there, walk past the "Tang Monk" stone, one of the park's most iconic rock columns, and through the Minor Stone Forest. The trail ends where it began, at Shilin Lake.

A less touristed section of the Stone Forest is Naigu Shilin Scenic Area, about 10 kilometers north of Shilin Scenic Area and next to the Tuanjie Reservoir. The area can be reached by bus from Kunming East Coach Station, and admission costs RMB 175, waived if you buy a ticket to Shilin. The main loop is about 1.5 kilometers, though taking the side trails can significantly extend it, and loops around such sights as Baiyun Lake, Baiyun Cave, Ancient Battlefield, Zhuge Liang's Eight Diagram Formation, and 9 karst caves. Another reason to visit Naigu is the fields of beautiful white-pink coreopsis flowers, which bloom each year from September to November near the entrance gate. These flowers are so dense that it seems the ground has been frosted. Naigu is much less crowded than the Shilin Scenic Area but no less grand, and is well worth a little hiking time.

HIKING IN YUNNAN

THE EAST

Hiking in the Shanghai Area

Xi Hu (West Lake) 西湖

Xi Hu, literally West Lake, is a lake and UNESCO heritage site in Hangzhou, Zhejiang province, a little south of Shanghai. The lake is known for its many historic landmarks, pagodas, and gardens, which have inspired Chinese literati for centuries. In the early 9th Century, a poet and governor of Hangzhou named Bai Juyi described the lake:

> "North of Lone Hill Temple, west of the Jia Pavilion,
> The water's surface has just smoothed, the foot of the clouds are low.
> Wherever you go, new-risen orioles jostle for the warmest tree:
> What are they after, these newborn swallows that peak at the spring mud?
> A riot of blossoms not long from now will be dazzling the eyes,
> The low grass can hardly yet submerge the horse's hooves.
> Best beloved of all, to the east of the lake, where I can never walk enough,
> In the shade of the green willows, is the causeway of white sand."

Besides poetry, the mythic scenery has inspired many

THE HIKES

tales, among them China's Legend of the White Snake, one of China's four great folktales. The story has been adapted into many operas, plays, and film series, and takes place at two of China's best-known landmarks, Mount Emei, and the West Lake's "broken bridge." The bridge is not actually broken, but when fog covers the water, the middle can disappear into the mist, seemingly incomplete. Visit in the early morning if you want a chance to see this phenomenon for yourself.

The story of the White Snake has many variations and extensions. The basic storyline begins with a young scholar Xu Xian passing by the Broken Bridge one day in the rain, when he notices two ladies without an umbrella huddled under a willow tree. Unbeknownst to Xu, the lady Bai Zuzhen is really the embodiment of a white snake spirit, and the lady Xiaoqing, the spirit of a green snake, is her companion and servant. Seeing them without an umbrella, Xu gives them his, and thus becomes acquainted. He and Bai Suzhen eventually fall in love and are married. But a Buddhist monk named Fahai discovers the union and decides to break them apart, either because he disapproves of relations between a human and a spirit or because of jealousy, depending on the story. Fahai imprisons Bai Suzhen or Xu Xuan, but they eventually break free to be with each other.

How to Get There

You can travel to Hangzhou from Shanghai by bullet train in under an hour. From Hangzhou East Station you can reach West Lake in about twenty minutes by car or by subway. Consequently, the lake and the surrounding scenic area are readily accessible from the city, and so you can stay at any of the numerous hotels and hostels Hangzhou has to offer, or even make the excursion a day trip from Shanghai, if you wish.

Trails
The West Lake Loop is probably the most popular trail around the lake. Encircling its perimeter, the path is an 11-kilometer closed loop, taking visitors through some of the more famous sites. This section of the park is heavily trafficked, so don't be surprised to see large numbers of people flying kites, walking dogs, or practicing Tai Chi along the way. Despite the number of visitors, this section is worth taking if you have the time, because it has not only some of China's best-known historical landmarks but also shows how Chinese people enjoy the West Lake in the present day.

Another possible hike for those looking for more tranquility and less people begins at Yanggong Causeway. From there, hikers can go through Maojiapu Village, with buildings in a classic Chinese architectural style. From there walk through the Hangzhou Flower Nursery, and then the Crooked Courtyard, which in the 12th and 13th centuries was once a winepress and later became famous for lotus blossoms. Head on to Guo Village, and then the Hangzhou Botanical Garden, where in season you can enjoy the lotus, peach, and plum blossoms for which West Lake is known.

Moganshan 莫干山
A mountain forest retreat a few hours from Shanghai, Hangzhou, and Nanjing, Moganshan is known for being a calming weekend retreat for urbanites eager to escape

the summer heat. First settled by missionaries in the late 1800s, Moganshan has hosted foreigners, politicians, and even gangsters for more than a century. By 1910, the area had accumulated about 300 Western expatriates, most of whom built homes in a variety of Western styles. In 1927, Chinese President Chiang Kai-shek honeymooned here with his bride, Soong Mei-ling. Moganshan is popular today for many of the same reasons people visited it in the 20th century—the vast bamboo forests, tea fields, charming old stone houses, and miles of hiking paths. First time visitors to China may prefer to visit grander and more classic destinations, but resident hikers will appreciate the chance to get away from the hustle ands the bustle of the city and lose themselves in this 43 square kilometer nature reserve.

How to Get There
You can hire a private car to take you from Shanghai, which will take about 3 hours. But there is also a bus that leaves the Old North Bus Station, which takes about 4 hours and leaves 3 times a day. Or you can take a train to Hangzhou, which takes up to two hours, and then take a taxi to Moganshan, about an hour away or less. You can also take a train direct to Deqing, which is closer to Moganshan. From Deqing, take a taxi or bus 113 for the final leg to Moganshan.

In terms of accommodations, many of Moganshan's old country houses and villas have been renovated into hotels, but due to the proximity to Shanghai staying at some of them can come with a hefty price tag. Guesthouses and budget lodgings are also available, so do your homework before you arrive to find a place to stay. Rates in the off-season tend to be much cheaper, so take that into consideration. Entry to the Moganshan Scenic Area costs RMB 80.

When to Go
The best time of year to visit Moganshan is in the spring and autumn, when the weather is cooler and there are fewer tourists. Winter, when snow blankets the mountain, is also an interesting time to visit, and entrance tickets are half-price. Avoid July through August, as this is when the weather is hottest and there are the most visitors.

Trails
A popular and short trail leads to the Sword Pool (剑池). Starting at the Sanjiuwu trailhead north of Shiyisi, walk north along the wood-lined path, following the signs. In a short ways you will reach the parking lot which tourists use to reach the waterfall area. From here, you can take the loop that goes down to the pool and then climb back up. The stairs can be slippery, so watch your footing. Legend has it that the Sword Pool is where two swords named Moye and Ganjiang were forged by a pair of husband-and-wife swordsmiths. After the swords were finished, he cut off their heads so they could not be replicated, and the mountain was subsequently named in their honor. Along the trail there are several statutes and calligraphic graffiti dedicated to the store, along with streams and cascades. When you have reached the pool and have had a chance to enjoy the water and the shade, return the way you came. This trail is a short 2.5 kilometers, and should take a couple hours.

A second, longer 6 kilometer hike loops around the top

THE HIKES

of the mountain. Walk north along the stream, and then through the bamboo forest. At the 1-kilometer point, the trail splits. Head left towards the viewing platform at the peak, 719 meters above the mountain's base. From here, you can get a good view of the surrounding mountain slopes and the valley. The dirt path then slopes gently down again, heading back into the bamboo forest. It passes through Dazaowu Village, many of whose stone houses were built in the early 20th century. From the village, the trail threads between two high hills for 1 kilometer, back to the trailhead. If you want to hike a bit further, you can add the Mogan Little Waterfall Loop to your route. It follows the same trail, but heads north to the right at the fork at the 0.6 kilometer mark, continuing up the valley to a waterfall before looping back for a total of 3 kilometers of extra trail.

The Moganshan area is threaded with paths, cycling paths, fields, and forests. There are many more hikes than the two included here. If you have the time, check out the areas around Da Dou Wu Reservoir and the Dakeng scenic area. The official information center can also provide you with maps and more information on trails you might want to take and places to visit.

The Anji Grand National Bamboo Forest
中国大竹海

Despite close proximity to Shanghai, the Anji Bamboo Forest is a calm weekend getaway that few tourists know about. Watchers of Chinese movies, however, might recognize the area as the filming site of the famous bamboo-grove fight scene in the movie "Crouching Tiger, Hidden Dragon." Practicing kung fu on this hike is optional, but visitors will enjoy peace and quiet in one of China's most precious ecosystems, and the enchanting sound of the wind rustling millions of bamboo leaves.

How to Get There
Direct buses to Anji City leave Shanghai's South Railway Station Bus Terminal regularly, and reach the town in about four hours. You can also take a train to Hangzhou, about two hours, and then take a bus from there. Once you arrive in Anji, you can take a taxi to the bamboo forest in about half an hour. Agree on a time for the driver to pick you up if you'd like. The entrance fee is RMB 55.

As for the return trip to Shanghai, the last direct bus leaves early in the afternoon, so it's best to rent a room in a local hotel and return early the following morning. If you are willing to spend a little extra time traveling, however, you can catch a bus to Hangzhou, and then take a bus or train north to Shanghai from there.

When To Go
The Grand National Bamboo Forest is open year-round. In fact, winter can make an interesting alternative to summer, especially if there is snow on the ground. Of course, the sunnier months in spring and autumn are good times to plan a trip, as the visibility of the valley will be better when it isn't raining and the trails less slick. In April, you can see farmers in the tea fields harvesting leaves.

Trails
The main path to the top of the mountain is an easy climb, about 1 kilometer. Along this trail you can see "Hidden

THE HIKES

Dragon Waterfall," and climb a viewing platform that provides a bird's-eye view of the valley, 60,000 hectares of bamboo forest, among the largest in China. The path itself is an easy hike, though fallen leaves and mountain streams can make some areas slippery. The forest is relatively untouristed, but you'll nevertheless notice that many people have carved their names in the tall bamboo plants. For a touch of excitement, there is also a toboggan course down the mountain on which you can negotiate a ride for about RMB 50. Even though the trail itself is short, spend some extra time wandering the bamboo groves and enjoying their tranquility.

Another attraction in Anji are the tea gardens. The area is known for its hills of tea bushes, and for the rare Anji White Tea (安吉白茶), which is actually a misnomer as the tea is actually classified as a green tea. This kind of tea is only planted in Zhejiang Province and has a strict harvesting period, making it one of the most expensive teas in China. Another local specialty is, unsurprisingly, dishes made with bamboo. The restaurants outside the forest entrance gate serve a variety of dishes made with the local plant, which is an excellent lunch opportunity.

HIKING IN THE SHANGHAI AREA

Hiking in Shandong

Taishan Mountain 泰山 and Qufu 曲阜

Of the Five Great Mountains of China, Taishan Mountain represents the cardinal direction of the east. Mount Taishan is the holiest and most accessible of the five, meaning it is visited by more than 6 million climbers every year. In Chinese tradition, it is associated with birth and regeneration. For this reason, people often hike up the mountain at night to see the sunrise with the aid of a headlamp, but as this makes it impossible to see the scenic views and monuments visible in the daytime, it is suggested that if you want to see the sunrise that you stay in one of the hotels near the top.

How to Get There

The access point for Taishan is Tai'an city, quite close to Qufu, about halfway between Beijing and Shanghai. Visitors to Taishan Mountain will likely pass through Qufu City on their way to Tai'an City as it is the major town in the area where the trains from Beijing and Shanghai stop. Beijing South Station to Qufu East Station takes less than 2.5 hrs and costs about RMB 250 for a second class ticket. The highspeed train does make a stop at Tai'an 20 minutes before reaching Qufu. Tai'an is less than 90 minutes north of Qufu, by bus or car.

THE HIKES

When to Go

The best time to visit Taishan is in the spring and autumn, when the weather is more temperate and the crowds less intense. Winter is also an interesting time to climb since there are far fewer people and the vistas are clear, but of course, the weather is very cold.

Trails

In terms of hiking paths, there are and eastern and western route up to the midpoint at Zhongtianmen, literally Midway Gate to Heaven. From Tai'an city you can take bus 3 or 9 to the eastern trailhead, or you can walk the same way along Hongmen Road in about 20 minutes. To reach the western trailhead, you can take bus 3 to the stop at Tianwaicun. This route is less crowded, so better for daytime hikers. The entrance ticket is RMB 125, but only RMB 62 for students with a valid ID card. Since so many people climb at night, the preserve is open 24/7.

Climbing to the halfway point will take about 2 hours, and another 2 to reach South Gate to Heaven, where most people stop. Another hour and you will reach Jade Emperor Temple, the highest point on this mountain of about 1,545 meters. In total, the trail is about 8 grueling kilometers. From Zhongtianmen, the path is a paved stone stair of 6,666 steps that rise 1,400 meters from the entrance to the top. Expect strong winds the nearer you get to the summit. If you simply want to attempt the 6,666 steps between Midway Gate to Heaven and the South Gate to Heaven (six is a lucky number in Chinese), you can take a bus to Zhongtianmen for RMB 30.

Taishan has 3,000 years of history, and has accumulated

many fantastic legends, such as that of Taishan Wang, god of the mountain and judge of the underworld, patron of the Dai Temple Complex at the mountain's base. Over the years, Taishan has been visited by many dignitaries. Qin Shi Huang, the first emperor of China buried in the mausoleum guarded by the Terracotta Warriors, supposedly announced the uniting of China officially from the summit in 200 B.C. Mao Zedong also climbed Taishan, declaring famously at the top that the east is red. Each pilgrim has left their mark on the mountain, from sacrifices in prehistoric days to the sacred graffiti caligraphy, embossed in red in modern times, which can be seen every few stone's throw along the trail.

Visitors to Taishan should also attempt to spend some time in Qufu City. Qufu is famous as the birthplace of Confucius, China's most famous philosopher and ethician. There is a major temple in the city dedicated to him which is worth a visit. Hikers seeking fewer tourists and a more natural scene to contemplate the sage should visit the Cemetery of Confucius, where his body, along with thousands of his descendants, is buried. From the temple, walk 1.5 kilometers north along Gulou Jie Road, which is the north-south axis of the Old City. After passing through the northern gate, the gate becomes Beiguan Jie. In 20 minutes you will reach the cemetery, filled with cypress and pine trees. It's worth taking some time to wander between the stone tablet grave markers and the carved statues, as well as viewing the grave of Confucius himself. The cemetery is open 8:00 am through 6:00 pm April to June, and closes at 6:30 July to October, 5:30 November to March.

The Penglai Vineyards

The Penglai area has a colorful and eclectic story to tell, including a Taoist philosopher who spoke to Ghengis Khan, a Scottish castle, and China's nascent wine industry. On the Shandong Peninsula on China's northern coast, Penglai is about an hour and a half by car from Yantai, which recently became accessible by both high-speed rail and an international airport. Penglai's history over the past couple of centuries is in many ways characterized by its contacts with the West, especially since the end of the Second Opium War when China was forced to sign the Treaty of Tianjin in 1858, opening seven new ports to foreigners. One of those ports was Penglai, and later nearby Yantai. Foreign involvement turned an area characterized by fishing villages into a colonial port town, with European architecture, much of which exists to the present day.

One of Penglai's most famous sons and best known traveler is the Taoist philosopher Qiu Shuyi, or Qiu Changchun, for whom Qiu Mountain is named. In 1219 the famous warlord Ghengis Khan wrote the philosopher a letter, asking to meet with him. Qiu obliged, traveling through modern Mongolia and Afghanistan to where Ghengis was camped near the Hindu Kush, a journey of thousands of miles. There, he had twelve conversations with the great lord, and Ghengis asked Qiu Shuyi about obtaining an elixir of immortality. While he expounded on Taoist beliefs regarding extending life, Qiu was frank with the Mongol leader that no such medicine existed.

Remarkably, Qiu survived the encounter and travelled back to China with celebrity, and a temple was constructed in his honor. An account of his travels was written and published by his pupils a few years after his return, translated as "Travels to the West of Qiu Changchun." The account has some the most striking descriptions of Samarkand and other places between the Great Wall and Kabul. In the present day, Qiu Shuyi was immortalized out-of-character as a villain in Jin Yong's Kung fu novel *Legend of the Condor Heroes*, one of a famous Chinese epic fantasy series.

Qiu Shuyi might be Penglai's most famous globetrotter, but in order to understand Penglai's most famous landmark, we need to travel forward in time about eight hundred years. In 2004, a British gentleman named Chris Ruffle showed up in Penglai looking for about forty acres of land. A developer was going to turn the plot he had in mind into a golf course but Ruffle had other ideas. He purchased the land, and then planted grapevines to make wine, something of a novelty in China. Few Chinese prefer grape wine as an alcoholic beverage, and almost all wine is still imported. Ruffle, an avid wine and China enthusiast, decided to change that. Not only did he establish Treaty Port Vineyards, but he built a replica of a Scottish castle on his land under the guidance of the premier architect Ian Begg with granite drawn from a local quarry. Visitors can spend time around the vineyards and book rooms for RMB 765 a night at the Scottish Castle, or at a hotel or hostel in Penglai town, such as the popular Runaway Cow Boutique.

When to Go

The rock formations around Penglai are granite, and the soil is volcanic. This makes the area ideal for a variety of agriculture besides grapes, especially fruit trees. Cherries, peaches, and apricots all grow in abundance in Penglai seasonally, and

THE HIKES

visitors should avail themselves of the fresh local produce. The best time to visit, therefore, is from May through June, and September through November. This avoids spring rains and the muggy heat of high summer. Fall is an especially fine time to spend outdoors in Penglai, as the weather is cool and dry and the farmers are bringing in the harvest.

Trails

One of the best hikes in Penglai is from the Ruffle castle, through the vineyards, and up Qiushan mountain. Upon leaving the castle gates, head right along the path to take a short detour to the temple dedicated to Qiu Chuyi, which currently has three monks in residence. After visiting, you can head left towards Qiushan mountain through the Lafite vineyards. Eventually, after passing the fields, you will head right down towards the village, and at the base of the hill reach a farmhouse which houses pigs and goats and also produces local honey. Here the trail starts up the mountain and then forks, the left hand going around the mountain at an easier grade, and the right heading more directly up Qiushan. As you hike up, enjoy glimpses of the Bohai Gulf to the North, and Aishan Hot Springs National Park to the south. Near the summit is an old wall built during the Nian Rebellion from 1851-68, when the Nian Army rebels were active in the area. The wall is a relic from a time when rebellions were sweeping China, most notably the Taiping Rebellion in southern China, but the dying Qing dynasty managed to hold on to power until the early 20th century. From this point, you can hike down the other side and circle back to the starting point, about two hours in total, 5 kilometers round trip.

HIKING IN SHANDONG

Hiking in Anhui

Yellow Mountains 黄山

The Yellow Mountains is actually a group of 70 granite peaks, eroded into fantastic spires. Also called the "mountain of 20,000 poems," the scenic area has historically inspired a myriad of Chinese poets, painters, and nature enthusiasts. Li Bai once described the Yellow Mountains in the first part of his poem, "Seeing-off Hermit Wen:"

> "Thousands of feet high tower the Yellow Mountains
> With thirty-two magnificent peaks,
> Blooming like golden lotus flowers
> Amidst red crags and rocky columns.
> Once I was on the lofty summit,
> Admiring Tianmu Pine below.
> The place is still traceable where the immortal
> Before ascending to heaven, made an elixir of jade."

The landscape looks like something straight from multiple Chinese paintings, with steep stone peaks cloaked in mist descending to roaring rivers. The Yellow Mountains are famous for their stunted pine trees, rapeseed flowers, and azaleas, clinging precariously to steep granite cliffs,

THE HIKES

as hikers are similarly liable to. The place names resemble those from a fantasy novel, and standing above the cloud-cloaked valleys it is easy to imagine oneself in a Chinese legend or film.

How to Get There
Four hours from Shanghai via train through Hangzhou, the Yellow Mountains remain as popular today as they have been for well over a thousand years, due in no small part to their accessibility. You can also get to the Yellow Mountains from Nanjing by train or bus.

When to Go
When planning when to visit, take into account when certain trails will be closed and when the tourist seasons are, which will lengthen lines, enlarge crowds, and increase prices. From December through March, the West Sea Grand Canyon, Celestial Capital Peak, and Lotus Peak are closed due to snow and ice. Peak tourist seasons are during the major holidays and summer vacation from July through August. Some of the best months to visit are March through April, when the mountain flowers are in bloom, and September through October when the fall-colored foliage peaks.

Trails
For a day hike that hits the major peaks, take the cableway from Mercy Light Pavilion to Yupinglou Cableway Station. From there, you can loop through Celestial Capital Peak, Lotus Peak, and Bright Top fairly easily before returning to the station. This loop will also take you past Greeting-Guest

Pine, an old tree famous for its welcoming shape. Bright Top is also a good location to see the sunset and sunrise if you decide to stay the night, and is near Baiyun Hotel. Depending on your condition and which scenic overlooks you decide to visit, expect this route to take 2-4 hours, with a full length of about 11.6 kilometers.

If you have more than one day to spend in the mountains, another suggested route begins by taking the cableway from Songgu Nunnery to Purple Cloud Peak. From there, head to flying-over rock, Bright Top, then the long trek to Fairy-Walking Bridge. While the bridge is worth seeing simply to take photos, be aware that it is not for those afraid of heights. Heading back from the bridge, turn right instead of left at the fork towards Haixing Pavilion. From there hike to Turtle Cave, the Hundred Ladders, Lotus Pavilion, and then Celestial Peak. From there you can take the Yuping Cablecar back to the base of the mountain. If you are staying overnight, consider Bright Top Hotel or the Bright Top Villa near the eponymous landmark, or Yuping Hotel near Lotus Peak and the cableway. This route is nearly 15 kilometers of pathways and steep stone stairs, so it is best to make it a two-day affair.

These are just a sample of the trails and famous overlooks hikers can see. Purchase a good map when you arrive at Yellow Mountain, and plan which of the trails and detours you want to attempt. It's easy to spend several days hiking and still not see every major temple, famous tree, statue and overlook, so work out where you want to go before setting foot on the trail. Also keep in mind that while technically, Yellow Mountain is not that high, the tallest point at Bright Summit Peak a mere 1,841 meters above sea level, the steep

THE HIKES

trails made of ancient, hand-cut stone stairs make many of the paths strenuous hiking. Make sure you are prepared physically, mentally, and for allowed for the amount of time it will take to get from one location to another. If you are planning on only spending one day at the park it is better to take one of the cable cars to begin closer to the peaks than to start at the bottom. Be aware that in peak seasons the lines for the cable cars will be quite long, due to the Yellow Mountains' widespread fame and popularity with tourists.

An additional treat awaits hikers at the bottom of the Yuping Cableway–hot springs. A 30-minute walk from Mercy Light Pavilion will take you to a natural hot spring resort famous for its refreshing and healing properties. Legend has it that the Huang Di emperor, for whom the mountains are named, bathed in this hot spring and recovered his lost youth. While it is doubtful whether modern visitors will become young again, the springs are a great way to end one or more long days in the mountains.

HIKING IN ANHUI

Hiking in Jiangxi

Lushan Mountain 庐山
Along with its natural attractions, Lushan is also a popular red tourism spot due to the Lushan Conference, which took place in the summer of 1959 at which the Great Leap Forward was discussed and Mao cemented his position within the Communist Party. The site of the conference is an easily accessible building in Guling. More broadly, Lushan has been a kind of summer resort destination for over a century, first for wealthy foreign merchants and for missionaries who constructed colonial-style buildings. Then for the Nationalist government leaders and then the Communist government leaders. Even Ho Chi Minh, the leader of the Vietnam Communist Party, at one time had a villa here. Political dignitaries and elites could bathe in the mountain's healing waters while contemplating the fate of nations. However, Lushan's history goes much further back in time, to the Han Dynasty two thousand years ago. Hikers with an interest in Eastern religions will also be interested to know that the monk Huiyuan built Donglin Temple on the mountain's slopes, and here founded the popular and powerful Pure Land Sect of Buddhism. As a result, Lushan is steeped in multiple layers of history that hikers can savor along with the beautiful mist-cloaked valleys.

THE HIKES

How to Get There

Lushan is a mountainous area at the junction of the Yangtze River and Poyang Lake. Because of its proximity to Nanchang, Jiangxi Province's capital, which is itself a 3 or 4 hour train ride from either Changsha, Wuhan, Nanjing, and Shanghai, Lushan is one of the most easily accessible scenic areas in eastern China. In order to get to Lushan from Nanchang, you can take a bus departing from in front of the Nanchang train station, a trip taking about 2.5 hours. You can also reach Lushan by train, the most convenient stop being Jiujiang Station, not Lushan Station. Regardless of whether you take a bus or a train, it is easy to take a shuttle from the intercity bus station about 1 kilometer north of the train station up into the mountains. The end destination of Guling Town has many hotels to choose from in terms of accommodation.

Trails

Instead of having one or a few main trails and scenic points, Lushan is covered in a web of trails that meander among touristy scenic areas, all connecting to the main tourist town, Guling, nestled in a valley in the center of peaks. Guling is at an altitude of about 1,000 meters, while the surrounding ridges climb to Dahanyang Peak at 1,500 meters, providing plenty of opportunities for mountain hiking. While often crowded, the town is worth some time in its own right. There are many old buildings in the European villa style, dating from when Lushan was a resort popular with foreigners, as well as many museums and historic sites.

One recommended hike is to follow Dalin Street down to Ruqing Lake, where you can wander around Flower Path

Park and see the Heavenly Bridge. In this area is a peak called Xian Feng, where couple like to hang locks from the trail rails to symbolize their love. From the lake, hike west to Fairy Cave, Imperial tablet Pavilion, and Heavenly Pool Pagoda. Here, the trail turns south to Dragon Head Cliff. A suspension bridge spans the river, and after crossing you can take a cable car back to the main road and catch a bus back to Guling. This path is under 5 kilometers, but due to the steep sections of the trails, it may take around 4 hrs.

Another, more strenuous hike goes to Sandiequan, the "Three-Step Waterfall, and Wulaofeng, or "Five Old Men Peak." From Guling, you can hike over the hills and across a valley to the ridge where these attractions are located, about 4 kilometers. Five Old Men Peaks is a rugged climb to 1,358 meters, but the views are worth it. In the same area is the waterfall inside a deep canyon, with 155 meters of falling water. You can climb to the second of the three tiers via a trail, or take a cable car. Both the peak and the waterfall are classic sites of Lushan, but because they are farther by road from Guling than some of the other sites, there are fewer tourists on the trails.

If you have some extra time and want to rest for a bit, one of the more unusual activities available is to watch a movie. In Lushan City's center, there is an old theater with an auditorium that is unchanged since its first opening. For thirty years, this theater has shown only a single movie, "Romance in Lushan" (庐山恋), a Guinness World Record. There are no English subtitles but the plot of this film movie from 1980 is easy to follow, a Romeo and Juliet-esque affair between two lovers who belonged to different parties, the Communists and the Nationalists. Scandalous back in

THE HIKES

the day for amongst other things featuring a kiss, the film touches on a number of topics that complicated its release. It is one way to learn about Lushan's modern history that doesn't involve a museum collection.

Sanqingshan Mountain 三清山

Mount Sanqingshan is usually less crowded than Huangshan and Lushan, despite being a UNESCO world heritage site as well as one of China's National Geoparks. The name comes from the three main peaks of the mountain, Yujing, Yushui, and Yuhua, which represent the Three Pure Ones, the most important figures of the Taoist pantheon. Rather than gods, the three are actually manifestations of heavenly energy, but are often depicted as three elderly men in religious paintings. The highest peak, Yujing, is 1,817 meters above sea level. Sanqingshan is also remarkable for its diversity of flora and fauna. Within the park's 229 square kilometer area live more than 2,300 species of plants and 400 species of vertebrate animals. Unlike many other Chinese mountain destinations, Sanqingshan is still relatively unknown, at least for the present, making it a great destination for hikers who want history and natural scenery with somewhat fewer trail mates.

How to Get There

From Shanghai, it's a 3-hour train ride to Yushan South Station. You can take a taxi to the bus station. Buses to the base of the Jinsha Cableway at Sanqingshan run every 40 minutes, and the trip takes less than an hour, but the road conditions can be quite intense and the vehicles old, so fasten your seatbelt. Admission tickets to the park cost about RMB 150. Accommodations are available at a range of prices on the south side of the mountain. There are also hotels within the park, both near the cable cars and at the top, but they are significantly more expensive.

When to Go
Because of its location in China's southeast, Sanqingshan is accessible all year round. However, in winter the steep and narrow stone trails can be icy and dangerous, so it's best to keep to the easier paths at that time of year. In late spring, the mountain flowers will be in bloom, which can add a special touch to the sheer rock faces and their hardy vegetation. Stunted rhododendron trees bloom from May to June, giving the mountain air a sweet tinge.

Trails
The trails on Sanqingshan have a variety of terrain, from long stretches of mostly flat paths to narrow stone stairways next to vertical drops. You can hike up the mountain and then begin the main trails, but it will take over two hours and may not leave you with enough time or energy to see all the scenic overlooks. For this reason, it is recommended that you take one of the two cableways to the top, either the Jinsha Cableway or the Southern Cableway, which will cost a few hundred RMB per person. In the summer, the cableways run until 6:00pm, and until 5:00pm in the winter. If you miss the last car, you might have to purchase a rather expensive hotel ticket, or hike down the steep stone trail in the dark.

First, take the Southern Cableway up the mountain. The endpoint of the car is still 300 meters lower than the

THE HIKES

main trail loops, so hike up the trail that passes west of Immortal Pointing The Way Rock, until you reach the West Coast Scenic Way, about 3 kilometers or 1 hour. At about 4 kilometers long, this route winds up and along a cliff face, offering fantastic views of Yujing Peak, and Tangseng Unfettered Rock (Tangseng is another name for the legendary monk responsible for bringing the Buddhist scriptures to China, Xuan Zang).

At the end of the West Coast Scenic Way, you should detour to take the loop around Sanqing Temple, about 2 kilometers. Sanqing Temple is a site not to be missed, and for this reason it is recommended you do the Western Coast-Sunshine Coast loop if you only have half a day. Arranged around the temple are various stone carvings. The site has about 1,500 years of history, although the current temple structure dates from the Ming Dynasty, 500 years ago. Ancient Taoists used to meditate here and grind elixirs of immortality. Though unmarked, the grounds are scattered with hidden treasures, such as statutes of tigers and dragons covered by mountain vegetation. The nearby lake is also quite picturesque, and makes a good place to rest or eat.

Once you are finished at the temple, head back along the Sunshine Coast Scenic Way, about 3.5 kilometers. This section consists of footpaths made of concrete steps often suspended in midair, joined to the cliff face with metal beams. While this hiking can be challenging, it has fantastic views of Yuhua Peak, Lush Pine Forest, and the ridge called Three Dragons Rising from the Sea. This trail will take 2 to 3 hours. Sun and mist can provide equally beautiful vistas, from clear views of wide valleys to the famous cloud cover that inspired Chinese ink wash paintings.

Another, longer hike is to do two loops. Start from the Southern Cableway and proceed as before, but when you get to the start of the West Coast Scenic Way, turn right and head north instead towards Beauty Peak and Pagoda Peak. This eastern loop of the park with take you past the famous Python Emerging From the Mountain rock formation, where a snake's head appears to rise from the mist. Continuing, you will pass the Immortal Goddess, and then turn south towards. Jade Platform. Eventually, you will loop back around to where you began, and you can now complete the loop towards Sanqing Temple as outlined above. The eastern loop will take 3-4 hours, and is about 3.5 kilometers.

THE HIKES

About the Author

Mable-Ann Chang was born in South Africa and has lived and worked in China for five years. As a journalist, she writes and edits feature stories on economics, policy and business in China and is a lover of the great outdoors.